S A C R E D
ARCHITECTURE

SACRED
ARCHITECTURE

A. T. MANN

ELEMENT

Shaftesbury, Dorset ❖ Rockport, Massachusetts ❖ Brisbane, Queensland

Text © A. T. Mann 1993

Compilation © Element Books Ltd. 1993

Published in Great Britain in 1993 by

ELEMENT BOOKS LIMITED

Longmead, Shaftesbury, Dorset

Published in the USA in 1993 by

ELEMENT INC

42 Broadway, Rockport, MA 01966

Published in Australia in 1993 by

ELEMENT BOOKS LIMITED for

JACARANDA WILEY LIMITED

33 Park Road, Milton, Brisbane 4064

Designed by Peter Bridgewater

Typeset by Vanessa Good

Printed and bound in Great Britain by the Bath Press

British Library Cataloguing in Publication

data available

Library of Congress Cataloging in Publication

data available

ISBN 1-85230-391-3

PICTURE ACKNOWLEDGEMENTS

BRIDGEMAN ART LIBRARY 28T, 132, 134, 135BL, 141T, 146, 147T, 149B, 167T/Archaeological Museum, Delphi 57B/Bibliotheque National, Paris/Giraudon 26, 45/British Library, London 12, 30B, 95, 123B, 159, 171/British Museum, London 13TR,/Fine Art Society, London 46/Fitzwilliam Museum, Cambridge 173T/Fratelli Fabbri, Milan 176/Galleria dell'Accademia, Venice 34/Giraudon 104T/Kunsthistorisches Museum, Vienna 11/David Lees 166-7B/Musee Conde, Chantilly/Giraudon 58T/National Museum of American Art, Washington/Art Resource 39B, 93B/National Museum of India, New Delhi 100B/National Museum, Stockholm 6/National Trust, Fairhaven 54/Prado, Madrid 154/St. John's College Library, Oxford 18/University of Oxford for the Bodleian 21/ By Courtesy of the Trustees of the Board of the V & A 27B, 76/Vatican Museum 16-17;

PAINTON COWEN 139TR, 142-3;

JULIA HANSON 9L;

HULTON DEUTSCH COLLECTION 10T, 10B, 22, 24-25, 27T, 28BL, 33, 38, 40-41, 42, 43TR, 43B, 55R, 56, 64T, 65T, 71TL, 87L, 91, 94, 98, 99B, 101B,112, 119B, 122B, 129T, 133R, 136, 148BL, 148BR, 156, 158, 168T, 170, 177BR, 178T, 179B, 181T, 181CR, 186T/Bettman 185T;

HONG KONG TOURIST ASSOCIATION 78B, 83;

IRISH TOURIST BOARD 60T, 61C, 61B, 62, 63B;

P KENT 31, 43TL, 44, 60B, 61T, 63T, 65B, 68, 88T, 101TR, 119T, 130, 138, 140L, 150, 151TL, 151BL, 152, 168B, 169, 174, 175, 178B, 180, 181B, 182, 184B;

A. T. MANN 28BR, 32T, 39T, 53, 66, 84, 92, 96T, 99T, 100T, 107T, 108T, 109B, 110B, 113B, 114, 118, 137, 139TL, 155, 157, 160, 163;

SPECTRUM COLOUR LIBRARY 7, 9R, 13B, 14, 15, 23, 29, 30T, 35, 36, 37, 40, 47, 52, 55L, 57T, 58B, 59, 64B, 67, 69, 70, 71TR, 71B, 73, 74, 75, 77, 78T, 79-82, 85, 86, 87R, 88B, 90, 93T, 96B, 97, 102, 103, 104B, 105, 106, 107B, 108B, 109T, 110T, 110-1, 113T, 115, 116, 120, 121, 122T, 123T, 124-128, 129B, 131, 133L, 135T, 135BR, 139B, 141B, 144, 145T, 148T, 151BR, 153, 162, 164-6, 172TR, 173B, 177BL, 179T, 185B, 186B, 187;

CHRISTIAN THAL-JANTZEN 183,184TL, 184TR

CONTENTS
• • •

INTRODUCTION

· · · · · · · · ·

6 THE BEAUTY OF THE UNSEEN FORM IS BEYOND DESCRIPTION – BORROW A THOUSAND ILLUMINATED EYES, BORROW. 9

JALALUDDIN RUMI

From the age of ten I wanted to be an architect, and although there were no architects in my family or within our circle, it became an obsession with me. From the beginning, architecture seemed to me to be the most perfect evocation of the sacred in life.

In my youth, trees fascinated me. I revelled in their beauty, climbed them and made them my friends. Others never seemed to understand them in quite the same way, so this secret worship remained personal and solitary for me. As a child I spent hours making little houses and shelters in the crooks of giant oak, maple, sycamore and other trees both in the towns in which my family lived and in the wilds of nature in upstate New York and Canada, where we spent holidays and weekends. To me there was a powerful magic invested in trees.

Stars were equally mysterious and magical. Often I would gaze at them from the treetops, seeing the constellations pass across the sky against the sweeping branches. I imagined that the trees were pointers which identified and activated the power of the stars. In some way unfathomable to me, the trees and stars constituted the grandest knowledge available in the world. What puzzled me was that no one else seemed to see this. While the churches and the skyscrapers of nearby New York City were certainly potent and breathtaking in their worldly grandeur, the true mystery lay in these natural domains.

Throughout my teens, I took every available but limited opportunity to investigate what seemed to be magical buildings – from the abandoned Victorian houses in town to the sprawling country houses along the New York State Finger Lakes. My grandfather was originally an engineer. He had mysterious drawings of family trees, and also possessed spheres and other brass instruments covered with the locations of the stars. I knew that they were used for navigation, but never quite understood how. He designed his own house late in life and I was then sure that the domain of architecture was somehow related to the stars and the trees.

When I entered Cornell University for a five-year architecture degree, I expected the magical quest I had discovered in trees and sky and buildings to be supported and my inquiries illuminated – and that the secrets of the sacred architects of the ages would be revealed. Year after year, in the presence of some of the greatest architectural minds in American practice and academia, I waited for just one of them to approach the subject I yearned to understand – the sacred basis of architecture – but none ever did.

I imagined that the geometric forms used by the Egyptians, Indians, Romans, Greeks and other early cultures had a profound mystical significance, but was consistently and stridently told that early architecture was simply a repository of 'more primitive' forms of design, only to be used as prototypes. While I knew that

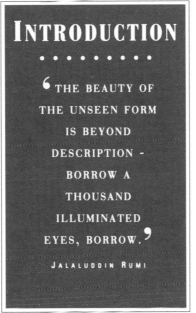

FIGURE 1 · ABOVE
The Duomo, Florence, Italy (begun 1294: Dome added 1420-36).

FIGURE 2 · LEFT
Planetary Trajectories, Anonymous. The movements of the planetary spheres were projected onto the heavens.

this logic supported the then modern International Style of architecture, which was in turn dominated by the principle of form following function, these ideas lacked depth and substance for me. I kept feeling that squares, cubes, rectangles and triangles were much more than simple geometric shapes to be played with and manipulated according to accepted stylistic lines. Certain shapes in specific buildings evoked deep feelings, ancient drives and powerful realizations, and I hungered to discover someone who acknowledged these ideas and illuminated their roots - but it was not to happen. A kind of shortsightedness seemed to have enveloped architects, regardless of their background or design orientation. Even the architectural historians ignored the sacred in architecture.

It was necessary to suppress my aspirations of discovering the magic of architecture, because we were required to play formal design games in which the winner was the one who could most effectively imitate Le Corbusier. Indeed some of the notable architects in the US and Europe are still playing this game, or have created its post-Modern manifestation as a shallow

gradient away from it. The lack of depth, it seems, is universal.

When I first visited Europe in 1964, I saw and felt the Italian cities as powerful and sacred places. Beyond their potpourri of styles and eras reaching back more than two thousand years, these cities evoked the mysteries in me. Somehow the vaults of great cathedrals, the domes of Florence, the Campidoglio in Rome, the space within the Pantheon, the frescoes of Piero della Francesca and the pristine shapes of Palladian villas in the Veneto brought the magic back. However, when I discussed these great buildings with my peers, I was rewarded by yet more gamesmanship about style. The great architecture of the past was perceived merely as a springboard for more formal gymnastics. Any mystical speculation was greeted with derision, and so I directed my questions within.

I had always imagined that an élite of architects existed, a group of celestials who really 'knew' the mysteries of architecture. After graduation, I was fortunate to be hired by a major New York City architectural office, and joined the American Institute of Architects. I met some of the giants of modern

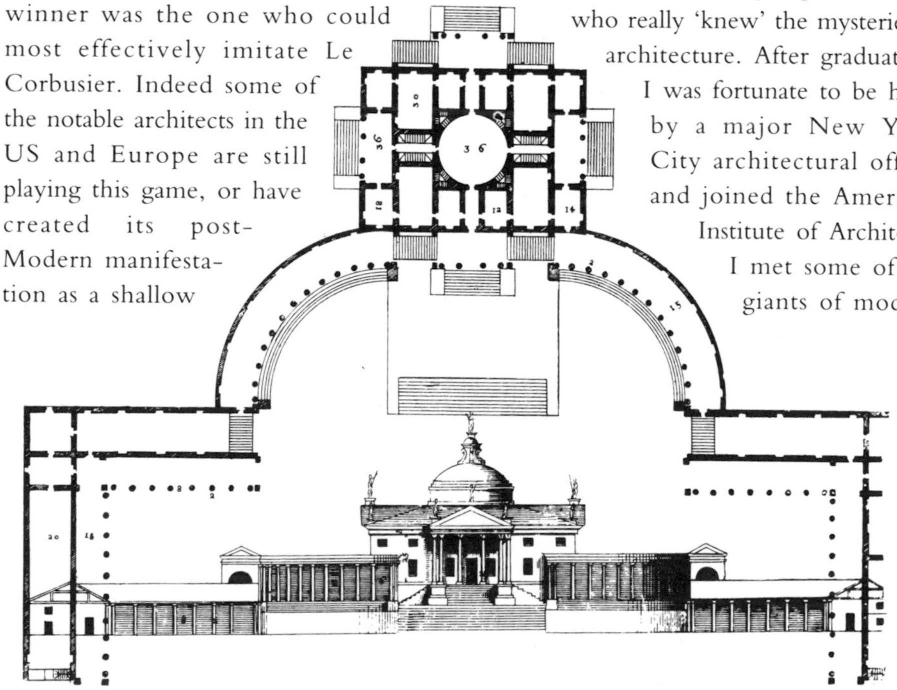

FIGURE 3 • RIGHT
Villa Trissino, Meledo, Italy, c.1552, by Andrea Palladio.

architectural design - Marcel Breuer, I. M. Pei, Philip Johnson and others. Having been taught by theoreticians influenced by the International School, I worked for offices which reflected this design philosophy, and eventually worked in Rome for the Bauhaus-oriented firm started by Walter Gropius, The Architects Collaborative. When seeking the magic in their designs, words or gaze, I found none. The old men lived off of the design ideas of dead styles; modified, spiced up and adapted by inspired college graduates. They made choices among the most informed options. The young lions plagiarized Le Corbusier then and are still doing so now, thirty years later.

Far from finding men who 'knew' of the sublime and magical foundations of architecture, I discovered that the notable architects I met or heard about were even further away from the core of architecture than I was. The same was true of the Modern movement in general. My classmates and contemporaries alike continued to produce pale imitations of Le Corbusier's deadly and vacant International Style buildings. In their publication photographs, made upon the completion of every building, they trotted in their own Corbusier chaise longues and Breuer sling chairs, the Mies van der Rohe glass tables and the Leger prints, and in the process recreated a dying and inef-

FIGURE 4 • ABOVE LEFT
*Taj Mahal, Agra, India
(1638-48).*

FIGURE 5 • ABOVE
*The Shah Mosque, Isfahan,
Iran (1612-30).*

FIGURE 6 • ABOVE
*Pythagoras (c.582-507 BC),
mathematician and philosopher.*

FIGURE 7 • ABOVE
*Plato (427-347 BC),
philosopher.*

FIGURE 8 • RIGHT
*Tower of Babel by
Peter Breughel the Elder
(c.1515-1569).*

fectual style, in which it was impossible to live. The more talented the copyist, the more successful he became. I felt like Howard Roark, the hero of *The Fountainhead*, Ayn Rand's book about an idealistic anti-establishment architect in 1930s New York who wanted to blow up buildings similarly 'redesigned' by his famous peers.

I had to leave the world of architecture to discover the first seeds of meaning in the field I love. A year in Rome, six months living in Morocco, a year travelling across central Asia to India and living in small Buddhist and Hindu temples on the edge of Himalayan lakes and Ganges shores awakened the magic for me again.

In an unsuspected way, the obsession with my new profession of astrology reactivated a quest to understand architecture and the mysteries of number, proportion and form, and provided the mystical tradition for which I had been searching in vain. I had always felt that the proportion systems in architecture were a vehicle for meaning and for communicating ideas, but my astrological ideas led me to realize that the three dimensions of traditional architecture (height, length and breadth) also included references to the fourth dimension, time. I discovered that the unique and mystical logarithmic proportions of planetary rhythms[1] corresponded to the basic mathematical structure of the human psyche, as Plato, Pythagoras and the Hermeticists had realized. Mythological undercurrents were prominent in the psychological matrix. Wherever my study took me, I found geometry and number as the primary source of magical thought. Magic

circles, mandalas and many meditation diagrams, as well as the sacred megaliths and circles, all had architectural origins and foundations. Some Indian yantra meditation diagrams are literally temple complexes as seen from above.

I had tapped into the sacred domain of architecture, but had to leave the practice of architecture in order to pursue its mystery. I found the lack of personal development was my greatest barrier, and remains the source of the primary separation between architects and everybody else. While psychologists and physicists have rediscovered and then accepted the reality of the unconscious, and then with difficulty integrated the concept into their personal and professional world views, architecture lags behind. However, the sacred tradition exists already within the pearl of architecture, awaiting its acknowledgement. With this book I return, refreshed by twenty years of study and professional practice, to my first love - the sacred in architecture.

This journey through sacred architecture will not be an encyclopaedic history. A selection of those works and buildings which are true monuments to the re-creation of the sacred will be analyzed and appreciated for their influence as catalysts and as representatives of a much wider and more pervasive tradition. Evidence of sacred architecture exists in virtually all cultures. I hope to inspire architects and others to re-discover and then re-invent the sacred in architecture in our time, when it has been diminished or eliminated from our lives. These concepts are intended to catalyse a 'New Sacred Architecture' which will stimulate and awaken our further consciousness of Gaia, the Earth Mother upon whom these temples have been and will be built.

It is essential to define the meaning of the word 'sacred' as applied to architecture. Sacred Architecture can mean many different things. 'Sacred architecture' is usually defined as a building or monument which has a religious function or uses the vocabulary of forms consistent with religious practice. The architecture I consider sacred is that which has a common root in the life of the soul and spiritual vision, rather than merely in forms which qualify as being religious. I am therefore more concerned with symbolism and meaning in architecture than with its aesthetics.

THE SACRED AND THE SYMBOLIC

....

6 THE SACRED LAND WAS GIVEN TO THEM BY THE GODHEAD, WHICH HAD SHAPED IT OUT OF THE REMAINS OF THE SUN AND THE MOON. 9

THE DAYAK OF BORNEO

This definition itself poses some problems because the 'spiritual' must also be defined. The spiritual is the active, dynamic aspect of the psyche, which is independent of forms, and yet is an essence which seeks expression in and through the world, always invested in forms. Those forms into which spiritual energy flow reflect a sense of the divine, and a science of such forms has developed throughout history, a science based on symbolism.[2]

There is an important difference between a 'symbol' and a 'sign', as Jung saw. A sign is a cipher, a mark standing for a discrete object or idea, such as the

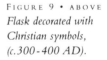

FIGURE 9 • ABOVE
Flask decorated with Christian symbols, (c.300-400 AD).

FIGURE 10 • FAR LEFT
Nasireddin's Observatory at Marega, Iran. Sighting the stars using astrolabes and other instruments in a specially designed building.

FIGURE 11 • LEFT
Mausoleum of the Galla Placidia, Ravenna, Italy (c.425 AD). The vaulted ceiling of the mausoleum represents the vault of the heavens, with sun, moon and stars.

IBM logo, a stop sign or a red telephone booth. Symbols, such as the church spire, the cross, or arch, carry living archetypal qualities and multiple layers of meaning.

Titus Burckhardt points out that symbols manifest archetypes according to definite laws, and express their essence through form.[3] Symbolic qualities evoke inner beauty and truth in a way which purely formal creation does not, or if it does, only does so accidentally. The great work of many architects is a fortuitous accident, a formal game which has evoked a solution beyond the architect's understanding. Symbolic architecture is based on principles which extend beyond

FIGURE 12 • BELOW
Paraporiani Church, Mykonos, Greece. The façade of a simple church represents the sacred mountain surmounted by a cross, and evokes stepped pyramids in its form.

formal rules, because they tap into the unconscious and mythic layers of being, and activate higher spiritual qualities.

• • •

THE MYSTERIES

• • •

Throughout history symbolism allowed the expression of multiple meanings – an outer meaning for the masses and a hidden meaning for initiates. There was always concern that the true spiritual principles would be discovered and abused by those interested in the pursuit of power. Egyptian religion, hieroglyphs and architecture incorporated a symbolic language; Jewish rabbis created the numerological system called the Kabbalah; the Pythagoreans concealed their philosophy in numerology and geometry; and the Gnostics used parables and poetry to communicate cosmic principles for which they would other-wise have been persecuted by the orthodox Church.

The true meanings of the symbols were understood by priesthoods and carefully kept secret from the uninitiated. Certain schools of artists and architects were trained by the priests to understand and communicate the symbolic through their work. The tradition of architectural secret societies, brotherhoods and guilds produced the master masons and work-men *(œuvriers)* who built the great cathedrals, and remains today in debased form as the masonic guilds. The symbolist tradition still exists to be seen in many monuments and buildings, some examples of which we shall be examining and exploring later in the book.

There are a number of ways in which the symbolic or the spiritual is expressed through architecture:

First, sacred architecture reflects the structure of the cosmos. Before there were buildings, humanity worshipped the stars and planets, the four elements, the earth, and its animals and plants, as gods. In our progression from caves to modern buildings, the symbolism of this early integration with the cosmos has been central, and still activates the deepest essence within us, the core of our psyche.

Initially, sacred monuments were associated with a particular god, goddess, or the natural or supernatural powers they represented. They were aligned by or with the stars or planets in the sky which represented the god or goddess. They were also geographically oriented and located in places significant to the gods. Some monuments were used by priests or priestesses as observatories to measure the movements of the planets or heavenly bodies they worshipped, while others were sited in accordance with planetary motions. Most megalithic monuments echoed some or all of these functions in their siting, design and function.

Second, sacred monuments were organized using primary geometric shapes and proportions, described by number symbolism. Mathematical mysticism or sacred geometry is a profound part of sacred architecture, and is often mentioned in relation to the Egyptians and Pythagoreans. Pythagoras created a humanistic philosophy which utilized mathematical harmony and proportion as primary tools in daily life, including art, architecture, music, morality and history. He believed that the order inherent in numbers, a number symbolism, creates specific effects on the observer, both psychologically and spiritually.

The discovery of the innate meaning of numbers is therefore a primary creative legacy of sacred architecture. The exploration of the numbers and proportions of the sacred brings a higher understanding to architecture.

Third, the sacred lives in buildings or monuments in which the structure and decoration follow clear and basic patterns derived from the ancient conception of the four elements, earth, water, air and fire, the forms of nature and from living energies and the geometries derived from them. Proportion systems amplifying

FIGURE 13 • TOP LEFT
Shah Mosque, Isfahan (1612-30). The blue floor tiles represent water, the source of life.

FIGURE 14 • TOP
Jantar Manter Observatory, Delhi, India. This observatory is astronomically sited and its form is determined by its uses. It is a three-dimensional astrolabe.

FIGURE 15 • ABOVE
Revolving Mausoleum, Kayseri, Turkey. A sacred building created using primary geometric shapes — the cylinder and the cone.

natural rhythms and patterns bring a natural and organic energy and spirituality to sacred architecture - the building contains an elemental as well as a human quality evoking the spiritual.

In time, the design criteria which gave certain monuments and buildings their sacred nature have been modified, forgotten, ignored, misused, misunderstood, stylized or eliminated from architecture as we know it today. This process has happened in such a way that *few modern architects even realize or acknowledge that the sacred ever existed, except in the formal sense of religious versus secular architecture.* Sacred architecture must therefore be considered an esoteric, that is *hidden*, discipline which needs to be rediscovered.

• • •

MYSTICAL MATHEMATICS

• • •

Let none ignorant of geometry enter here.

PLATO, THE REPUBLIC

A primary characteristic of sacred architecture is the importance of the measurements, proportions and geometry of a site and building. It is a symbolic language which communicates information beyond cultural or stylistic habits.

The square, circle, triangle and other primary plane shapes and their equivalent solid shapes (cube, sphere, pyramid) transcend historical, religious, cultural, civilizational and social influences - these shapes and their proportions are found in virtually all sacred architecture. They are the letters of a geometric vocabulary of architecture, and each has its own unique significance. A probable explanation is that when early civilizations discovered, measured and canonized solar, lunar and planetary cycles to create their calendars, it was natural to integrate the same

FIGURE 16 • RIGHT
The School of Athens, (1509-11), by Raphael (1483-1520). Vatican Palace, Rome. The mathematical organization of Raphael's fresco underlines the intimate relationship between geometry and philosophy. The figures at the top of the stairs to the left are grouped around Socrates. In the left foreground is Pythagoras, writing in a book, whilst on the right Euclid, compasses in hand, is drawing on a slate. Behind him are the figures of Ptolemy (in yellow) and Zoroaster, both holding globes – the one terrestrial, the other celestial.

FIGURE 17 • ABOVE
Detail showing Plato and Aristotle. The one points upwards, suggesting the existence of a higher, seemingly intangible reality; the other, downward gesture emphasizes the physical reality of the world.

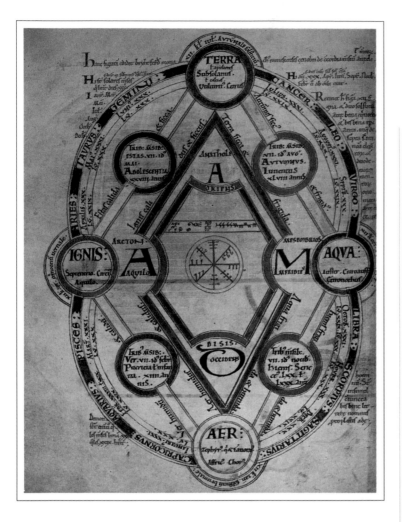

moon, planets and stars were gods and goddesses, and they determined the cycles of days, seasons, years and the larger cycles of world ages. Each deity was associated with a particular planetary body, and its activities and worship were related to the cycle of that body, the apparent measurements of the body, and any proportions used to describe its movements or position. To evoke the god, one had to create manifestations of the cycle or numbers associated with the related luminary, planet or star.

Rhythms sacred to the Moon goddess, often symbolized by her crescent crown, could be related to the lunar month, of which there were about thirteen in a solar year. The Egyptians utilized a fifty year cycle which reconciled the lunation cycle and the solar year by using the 'Golden Section' or *phi* (the proportion of 1:1.618). Fifty solar years contained

FIGURE 18 • ABOVE
Cosmological diagram from the Book of Byrhtferth, *(c.1110). A diagram showing the relationship between the four elements, the cardinal directions and the signs of the zodiac.*

FIGURE 19 • RIGHT
Spira Mirabilis. A spiral enlarging according to the phi proportion of 1:1.618 describes the growth of spiral shells, sunflowers and many other plants.

numbers, geometrical shapes and proportions into their sacred architecture which provided the temples in which to worship those same planetary deities.

The *Canon* was the ancient esoteric system of measurement common to many civilizations because it was derived in a similar way everywhere – the measuring scales came from an integration of planetary and human proportions. The Canon provided a mathematical standard which could be applied to music, art, architecture, sculpture, astronomy, government and the other arts and sciences. Plato believed that the Canon had been developed by the Egyptians and that it was a primary reason why the Egyptian civilization flourished for so many thousands of years.[4]

The development of sacred and symbolic numerology is natural. The sun,

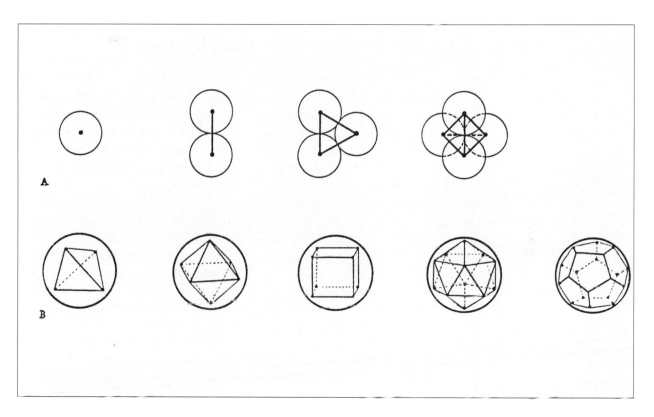

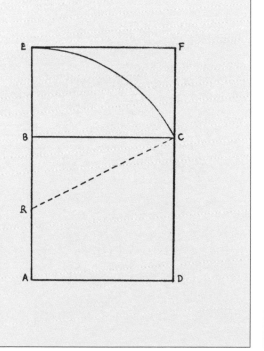

618(Φ) lunations.[5] The Egyptians believed that the possibilities for spiritual integration were greatly enhanced at the rare times when the solar and lunar calendars coincided.

The nineteen-year Metonic Cycle was celebrated as the time when new and full moons and solar and lunar eclipses returned to the same days of the year. The structure of the major circle of stones at Stonehenge was designed to keep track of this cycle.

Many such monuments were simultaneously calendars and astronomical observatories, integrating spirituality and science in early cultures. The numerology of planetary cycles infiltrated early megalithic monuments and subsequent architecture until it became inextricably integrated with the sacred. The number and the god became one.

FIGURE 20 • ABOVE
Platonic Solids. The regular solid shapes contained within a sphere define the mathematical movement through the dimensions of space, beginning with Unity. They correspond to the four elements and the sphere (Universe), as well as the chakras within the body.

FIGURE 21 • LEFT
The Golden Mean or divine ratio is produced mathematically when the side (AB) of a square (ABCD) is bisected at R and an arc with radius RC is swung on to AB at E. The resultant rectangles AEFD and BEFC are both golden rectangles whose sides conform to the Golden Mean, having the ratio 1: 1.618.

• • •

NUMEROLOGY

• • •

Pythagoras[6] (c.582–507 BC) was an initiate of the Egyptian mysteries in which number held the key to the world, and he explored the connection between the sequence of natural numbers and the structure of mind and the universe. Among his aphorisms were, 'All things are number' and 'God is a geometer'. The Pythagorean, Platonic and later Hermetic schools used the symbolism and interrelationships of numbers as their major logical teaching device.

Natural numbers have a significance beyond their function as quantities – they are also qualities with an archetypal symbolic meaning. It has been suggested that numbers are the most primitive element of order in the human mind, if not an archetype of order. Numbers are also spiritual and mystical in their own right. Humanity did not invent them, but discovered them as an integral part of reality, a statement which is in direct contradiction to the modern scientific view of numbers as merely quantities.

Pythagoras spoke of the 'music of the spheres', the planetary harmonies which govern the workings of the physical universe. According to him each number is a symbol possessing its own particular significance, mechanisms and harmonic relationships to other numbers.

Numbers participate in a continuum, a structure which unfolds in time, and contain meaning because they mediate between the physical and intellectual worlds (see Figure 22).

There are only five regular elemental solids which can be inscribed within a sphere, representing God, with all their apexes touching the sphere – they were

FIGURE 22 • BELOW
The meaning of the numbers. Each number carries qualities as well as quantity.

The number 1 is unity, singularity and existence. It cannot be multiplied or divided by itself because it is the divisor of all other numbers. It is a single point without dimension.

The number 2 is duality, which creates polarity in meaning. It divides, repeats and creates symmetries. Two points define a line of one dimension.

The number 3 centres the symmetries and initiates linear succession.[7] Three points define the surface of a plane figure of two dimensions.

The number 4 stabilizes through double or biaxial symmetry and turns back to the one, and corresponds to the four elements, the four forces of physics, and the four cardinal directions of the compass. Four points define a solid of three dimensions.

The number 5 is the four with a centre, and correlates with man. Inherent in the sequence of numbers are hidden and obvious harmonies, dissonances and an entire range of relationships. Five points define a solid moving through the fourth dimension of time, or the flow of psychic energy.

FIGURE 23 • LEFT
Hebrew Prayer Book (c.1501). The letters of the Hebrew alphabet symbolize concepts as well as being signs.

FIGURE 24 • BELOW
The sacred numerical attributions are shown left to right in Arabic numerals and letters, Hebrew characters and Greek characters. For example using this system, Fv=6, Tz=60, and X=600. The name of any being, object or deity can be determined by addition and every other name with the same sum would be of equal value and represent a similar quality.

• • •
GEMATRIA – SACRED NUMEROLOGY
• • •

Symbolic mathematics was at the core of the ancient mystery schools and determined the sacred principles which regulated people's beliefs and lives. While the nature of each god and its planetary equivalent could be represented by a number, the science of gematria attributed each letter to an equivalent number value. The system was integral to the Hebrew and Greek alphabets, but has also been applied to the Western alphabet. The numerical attributions[9] are shown in Figure 24.

By using gematria, the dimensions of temples and monuments, the verses in poetry, musical notes, rites and other

believed to be the form of the atoms which produced all things at Creation. Plato (c.427–347 BC) identified them with the five elements from which the world was made, and they have since been called the Platonic Solids. The tetrahedron was associated with fire, the cube with earth, the octahedron with air, the icosahedron with water and the dodecahedron with the universe because its surface was composed of twelve regular pentagons, corresponding to the signs of the zodiac. Every object, including of course the human body, contained a unique proportion of all five shapes.

Two thousand years later the great astronomer Kepler[8] (1571–1630) found that, when inscribed within spheres and within each other in sequence, the mathematics of the Platonic solids described the orbits of the planets in the solar system. Not for the first or the last time, the symbolic vision led to profound mathematical and scientific laws.

	ONES			TENS			HUNDREDS		
1	A	א	α	I	֝	ι	R	ק	σ
2	B	ב	β	K	כ	κ	S	ר	ρ
3	G	ג	γ	L	ל	λ	T	ש	τ
4	D	ד	δ	M	מ	μ	U	ת	υ
5	E	ה	ε	N	נ	ν	Ph	ך	φ
6	Fv	ו	ϝ	Tz	ס	ξ	X	ם	χ
7	Z	ז	ζ	O	ע	o	Ps	ן	ψ
8	H	ח	η	P	פ	π	O	ף	ω
9	Th	ט	θ		ץ			ρ	

FIGURE 25 • BELOW
Johannes Kepler, German
astronomer (1571-1630).
Kepler discovered that when
the Platonic solids were
inscribed within spheres and
then within each other, they
reflected the proportion of the
distances between the planets
in the solar system.

attributes could be correlated to the gods and their powers. It is possible to decipher any name or word and determine its deeper, symbolic qualities. Platonists, Hermeticists, Rosicrucians, Christian Gnostics, alchemists, masons, members of chivalric orders and many others utilized this sacred secret language. The entire Bible has been decoded using gematria - a science which is perceptual and spiritual in intention and practice, rather than materialistic.[10] There is an extensive literature describing the magical and psychological language of gematria.[11]

• • •

THE GOLDEN MEAN

• • •

The Golden Mean is a proportion found in nature - it governs the growth pattern and form of nautilus shells, the operculum (doorway) of the sacred molluscs revered in India, and many flowers, in particular the sunflower.

The magical qualities of the Golden Mean proportion, *phi* Φ, were central to the numerological philosophy of Plato and Pythagoras. It was used for the proportions of Egyptian and Greek temples, particularly the Parthenon. The pentangle was sacred to Pythagoras because it contains the *phi* proportion in its structure.

The mathematician Filius Bonacci (called Fibonacci) wrote a treatise on the number series related to the Golden Mean before Chartres Cathedral was built, and there is evidence that the builders knew about the Golden Mean formula and used it in the rose windows and the building itself (see Chapter 10). Pythagoras claimed that its proportions were musical, and it is true that the harmonious blending of musical intervals is governed by the series.[12] According to Helmholtz, fundamental tones described by this series create pleasurable consonances in the brain, possibly because analogous centres of the brain are affected by the visual nerves. Kepler called it the 'divine proportion'.

Architects have consistently used the divine proportion in their buildings, most notably in modern times the architects Le Corbusier and Frank Lloyd Wright.

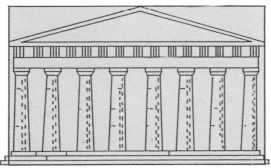

FIGURE 26 • ABOVE
*Parthenon on the Acropolis,
Athens (began 477 BC).
The proportions of the
Parthenon reflect the phi
proportion.*

FIGURE 27 • ABOVE
*Christ within the Vesica
Piscis illustration from*
The Benedictional of
St Ethelwold *(c. 908-984)
Bishop of Winchester shows
the Second Coming of Our
Lord within the vesica piscis
shape.*

FIGURE 28 • BELOW
*The Ely Vesica. Woodcut
of a vesica piscis in Ely
Cathedral, Cambridgeshire,
England.*

• • •

VESICA PISCIS

• • •

The Vesica Piscis was a figure often used by the mystery schools. The vesica is created by two interpenetrating circles, their conjunction being shaped like a lozenge. It is a symbol of the womb, the feminine principle, and the moon. In Christianity, the vesica symbolizes the Virgin as well as the spear wound in Christ's side. The Egyptians used it in their *crux ansata* cross. It was referred to by Plato, and used extensively by Dürer, Serlio and many architects of the sacred.

The double cube is also a common shape which is related to the vesica, and signifies the fourfold nature of the physical world. It is an irregular hexagon, with the proportions of 26 to 15, capable of containing a vesica piscis.

FIGURE 29 • LEFT
Glastonbury Plan. According to John Michell, the plan of the town of Glastonbury and the placement of the sacred buildings are organized according to the vesica piscis. (After The View Over Atlantis.*)*

FIGURE 30 • BELOW
The Bridge at Wilton House, Wiltshire, England, (1736). English architecture showing a combination of geometric shapes in neo-classical harmony.

• • •

REGULAR PLANE GEOMETRIC SHAPES

• • •

Like the Platonic Solids (see page 21), the regular plane geometric shapes can be inscribed within a circle with all their apexes touching the circumference.

The five-pointed star, the pentangle, which is inscribed within the pentagon, was the emblem of the Pythagoreans. The pentangle symbolizes the human figure with outstretched arms. Its numerology is the four elements, plus the additional human soul at the centre.

The primary Hebrew symbol was the six-sided 'Seal of Solomon' or 'Star of David', an intersection of two equilateral triangles, inscribed within a hexagon, which, among other things, contains representations of the four elements. The upward pointing triangle signifies the ascent of spirit and the downward pointing triangle is the descent of matter. The symbols of the four elements can be derived from this shape. (See Figure 31)

Virtually all cultures have used the cross in their religion, art and architecture. The cross has many variations, such as the equal armed as in the Delphic Cross, the upright cross of Jerusalem, the Egyptian Tau cross, often called the ankh, or the Byzantine cross with a diagonal crosspiece. The cross signifies the four cardinal directions and the cross of matter upon which the human is incarnated and the Christ energy crucified.

With a complete vocabulary of shapes, the artist and architect can create paintings, sculpture and buildings which correspond to the geometrical laws and thereby transmit specific meanings and qualities.

FIRE

AIR

WATER

EARTH

FIGURE 31 • ABOVE
The Seal of Solomon. The Seal of Solomon is two interpenetrating equilateral triangles which represents the physical world of the four elements as an integration of the spiritual impulse moving upwards and the physical reality moving downwards. The Seal breaks down into four triangles of the elements Fire, Air, Earth and Water.

In ancient times the temple was built as an image of god on earth, indeed it was believed to be the precinct or territory of the god.

Earth was believed to be flat and shallow, longer than its width, and the sky extended overhead like the immense iron ceiling of a barrel vault. As it could not remain suspended in space without some support, it was held in place by four immense columns, or pillars.

The floor of an Egyptian temple represented the earth; the pools and fountains

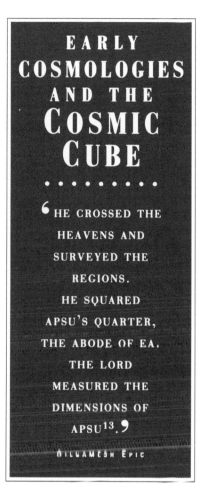

EARLY COSMOLOGIES AND THE COSMIC CUBE

• • • • • • • • •

❝HE CROSSED THE HEAVENS AND SURVEYED THE REGIONS. HE SQUARED APSU'S QUARTER, THE ABODE OF EA. THE LORD MEASURED THE DIMENSIONS OF APSU[13].❞

GILGAMESH EPIC

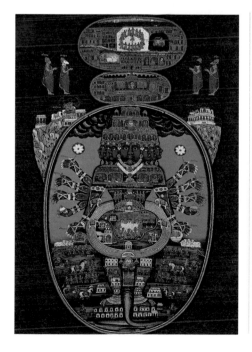

were seas and rivers; the arched ceilings the heavens. Each part was decorated in consonance with its meaning: those next to the ground were clothed with vegetation; the bases of the columns were surrounded by leaves; the lower part of the walls in Egyptian temples were adorned with long stems of lotus or papyrus, in the midst of which animals were occasionally depicted; and bouquets of water plants emerging from water fountains enlivened the bottom of the wall space in certain chambers. Elsewhere we find full-blown flowers interspersed with buds or tied together with cords.

The ceiling represented the sky and was naturally painted blue, spangled with five-pointed stars of gold and yellow. The goddesses of the winds, crowned and

FIGURE 32 • FAR LEFT
The Creation: God presenting Eve to Adam, by Josephe and Jean Fouquet, shows God with a compass and angels with t-square and surveying instruments.

FIGURE 33 • LEFT
Krishna in Cosmic Form, Rajasthan (19th/20th Century). The Hindus represented Shiva the Creator God within the Universe as a cosmic egg.

FIGURE 34 • ABOVE
Great Temple of Ammon, Egypt. In Egyptian sacred architecture, columns were abstracted bundles of reeds or papyrus, and the capitals were unfolding lotus blossoms.

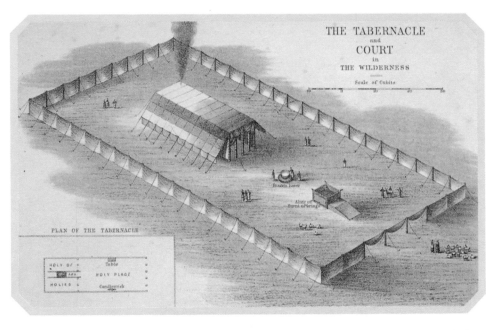

PLAN OF THE TABERNACLE

FIGURE 35 • RIGHT
Reconstruction of Solomon's Temple (19th-century print). The Tabernacle and Court in the Wilderness were created according to strict geometric shapes and proscribed dimensions.

FIGURE 36 • BELOW
Statue of Athena, Parthenon. A 19th-century reconstruction of the interior of the Parthenon shows the gigantic statue of the goddess Athena made of gold and ivory.

FIGURE 37 • BELOW RIGHT *Temple at Dendera, Egypt. The ceiling paintings show the rays emanating from the sun god Ra and the deities of the decanates crossing the night sky in their barques.*

FIGURE 38 • FAR RIGHT
Temple of Promaia Athena, Delphi, Greece (4th century BC). Early temples were often circular, reflecting the dome of the sky and the movements of the gods and goddesses.

armed with divine emblems, hovered above the central nave of the hypostyle halls and on the underside of the lintels of the front doors, above the head of the Great King as he passed through on his way to the sanctuary.

The representation of the firmament opened the eyes of the faithful, revealing the gods who populated the heavens. The luminaries, the sun and moon, passed across the sky, escorted by planets, against the backdrop of constellations and decans. All these were considered living spirits.

Even the genii of the months and days in procession were worshipped. In its use of doubled proportions the temple reflected the universe – the horizon separated above from below, the microcosm from the macrocosm, the heavenly from the earthly. Humanity lived at that intersection.

Solomon's Temple, the Jewish Tabernacle, the Athenian Parthenon, the Ka'aba ('cube') at Mecca, the Aztec sun temples and the Gothic cathedrals were all representations of sacred places, worshipped since the dawn of time, which echoed Paradise in the minds and hearts of those who entered these buildings. They contained the spirit and sacredness of our common origin.

FIGURE 39 • RIGHT
Tree of Life, Karnak Temple at Luxor, Egypt The Pharaoh is putting scarab cartouches on the Tree of Life, surrounded by the lion-headed goddess Sekhmet and the ibis-headed god Thoth.

FIGURE 40 • BOTTOM RIGHT *Norse Sacred Tree, title page from Reginald Knowles'* Norse Fairy Tales. *Norse legends and fairy tales centred around Yggdrasil the world ash tree, here shown with Odin as an eagle in its branches and the three Fates spinning the web of time at its base.*

Originally the temple was the dwelling place of the god or goddess, who was represented therein by a statue, a mystic symbol or invisible oracle. At the sanctuary to the prophetic god Apollo at Delphi, the temple covered what had originally been a fissure in the rock. The edifice was the image of the celestial dwelling, and the statuary and symbols showed the divinity which inhabited it. They were parts of the sky brought down for the use of humanity on earth, marking the sacred places where the gods spoke to their worshippers and acted.

All over the globe, people have created places which have intentionally evoked the sacred. The quality of the reflection was a gauge of the magical efficacy of the monument. And there is always an identification between the centre of the sacred precinct and the human psyche.

The form of temples reflecting the circular vaulted dome of the sky gradually metamorphosed from a cosmic monument or stone circle beneath the sky, representing astronomical principles within the precinct of the king, to a temple which contained and centralized the sky. Just as the spokes of a wheel are connected simultaneously both with the hub and the rim, so all creatures, all gods, all worlds, all organs are bound together in the temple of the world soul.

• • •

THE TREE OF LIFE

• • •

Early humanity recognized the sacred in natural places: initially in the sky, but later they also found representations of the heavens in trees, beside streams, inside caves, then, in tents or buildings.

Legends of the 'World Tree' abound in many cultures, such as the Tree of Good and Evil in the Garden of Eden, the Tree of Life of the Hebrew mystical

Kabbalah, the sacred oak groves of the Druids, and the Yggdrasil world ash tree of the Norse myths. Branches arching out into the sky and gigantic roots digging deep into the ground seem to symbolize the integration of heaven and earth.

Early Chaldean myths mention a tree at the centre of the world, the tapestry of which revolved to describe Creation. The Norse world ash tree Yggdrasil rises up from the centre of the earth, its branches forming the heavens of the gods and its roots striking down into hell where a serpent is entwined at the world's dark core. The Yggdrasil tree represented the fate of the world and determined the welfare of the universe. Beneath it lay the Well of Fate, *Uroarbrunnr*, where the female Fates, who laid down the courses of man's lives, were conceived.

Many images of the world tree seem fanciful to us, but they express the need felt by early humanity to make tangible the connection between earth and heaven. The tree is a powerful metaphor as expressed in ancient mythologies. Phenomena of nature and qualities of humanity are described in relation to the tree. Rain comes through holes in the fabric of the world tree. If one climbs high enough, one can ascend to heaven. The various regions of the tree's growth symbolize places where men and their souls exist. It is as though the universe was seen as a giant tree-house wherein humanity, the angels, the gods and devils all live, their domains determined by their various levels, all connected as a vast, eternal living organism.

This early stage of our evolution lasted for so many thousands of years that these concepts seem to have become an integral, if unconscious, component of later buildings, whatever their historical era.

THE PRECESSION OF THE EQUINOXES

One of first issues to be solved when building monuments to represent the heavens is their alignment. Most early monuments and temples were aligned to the luminary, planet or star corresponding to the deity to be worshipped. The rising, setting and other movements of the moon governed the orientation of lunar cult places and temples, while the correspondent positions of the sun determined solar places.

A difficulty in the alignment of monuments such as Stonehenge or the Great Pyramid is the Precession of the Equinoxes. The rotation of the earth around its polar axis creates day and night. However, the earth's axis is not perpendicular to the plane of the solar system, but is inclined at an angle. This inclination of the polar axis is what creates the seasons. The axis points the northern hemisphere towards the sun during the summer and away from it during the winter. At the equinoctial points in March and September, it points along

FIGURE 11 • BELOW
Precession of the Equinoxes. Due to the Precession of the Equinoxes, in 16000 BC the Vernal Equinox coincided with zero degrees of the astrological sign Sagittarius. The precessional point moves about one zodiac sign every 2,160 years.

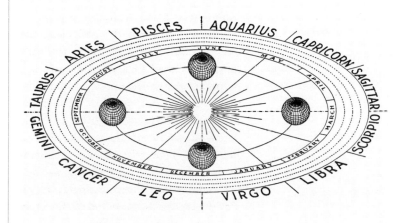

FIGURE 42 • ABOVE
Polar Constellations. The Pole Star, around which all the stars rotated, was often surrounded by the constellation Draco the Dragon, symbolizing time.

FIGURE 43 • TOP RIGHT
Mexican Calendar, showing 365 days in the year, phases of the moon and other solar divisions.

FIGURE 44 • BOTTOM RIGHT *Horus and Set Drilling. The falcon-headed Horus and the jackal-headed Set in the act of drilling or churning. This spinning creates both life and death.*

the axis and the seasons are equal in both hemispheres. The earth's axis also 'wobbles' like a top twirling slightly off centre, further increasing its irregularity.

At the present time the polar axis points to Polaris, but this has not always been so. The wandering of the axis produces a slow passage backwards in a westerly motion. The Spring Equinox is defined as the point when the length of the day is exactly equal to the length of the night, and the sun passes the equator along the ecliptic. This point is designated 0° Aries, and originally coincided with the beginning of the constellation Aries. The Egyptians discovered that the equinoctial point did not always correspond to the first zodiac sign, and after years of careful observations found that the equinoctial point moved backwards through the zodiac.

The complete revolution through the signs of the zodiac takes about 25,000 years, and is called a Platonic Year. The Spring Equinox pointer moving backwards through the signs creates a succession of Platonic months, each lasting 2,160 years, and only coincides with the beginning of the constellation Aries once every 25,920 years. The Greek astronomer Hipparchus (born about 180 BC) suggested making the Spring Equinoctial point always equal to 0° Aries, regardless of the actual constellation it occupies, a practice which both astronomers and astrologers follow to this day. Some astrologers, particularly those in India, still use the Sidereal Zodiac which continues to align with the constellations.

At present the equinoctial point is in the process of leaving Pisces, where it has been for the last 2,000 years, and entering Aquarius, where it will be for the next 2,000 years. Exactly when the change-over, which should radically transform the world, will occur is disputed, but many believe it will happen in or around the year 2000 AD. Such shifts of world age often produce dramatic events, such as the birth of Jesus Christ at the beginning of the Age of Pisces.

The world ages are major divisions of the history of humanity, and have been known and considered significant for thousands of years. The star towards which the earth's pole points is also significant and symbolic. For example, in the time of Ancient Egypt the pole star was Alpha Draconis, and the descending passage of the Great Pyramid pointed at Alpha Draconis when it was built. In our time the pole star is Polaris. The movement of the precession is approximately one degree every seventy-two years.

• • •

THE POLAR AXIS SPIRAL

• • •

The unusual movement of the earth's axis is a central factor in many of the early mythologies,[14] described by images such as a mill grinding on its axis, a wheel of fortune, the wheel of karma, or the churning of dairy products in the Milky Way. The ancients also likened the world to an egg surrounded by the *ouroboros* snake, symbolizing time.

The spiralling of the earth's polar axis is expressed in many creation myths. In the Aztec culture the axis is a fire stick, in Scandinavian myths it is Amlodhi's spinning top, and Egyptian stone carvings depict Horus and Set in the act of drilling, thereby creating the gods of the Nile. Indeed the Nile was often represented by the Egyptians as a circle, where its source and mouth meet like the *ouroboros*. The mill relates common mythological themes to the movements of the cosmos above, a central heritage of ancient philosophy. Coincidentally, the spiralling millstone and its cap containing hierogylphs look like human sperm containing the genetic code DNA.[15]

The central element of the mill is a pillar which grinds out reality, and the mill tree is also the axis around which the world itself is created. The form of the mill is central to the structure of eastern temples as described in the famous books of the East such as the *Ramayana* and the *Mahabharata*.[16] Similar symbolism is illustrated in Mayan Codices and in architectural friezes depicting churning objects which look like hour-glasses.

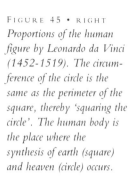

Proportions of the human figure by Leonardo da Vinci (1452-1519). The circumference of the circle is the same as the perimeter of the square, thereby 'squaring the circle'. The human body is the place where the synthesis of earth (square) and heaven (circle) occurs.

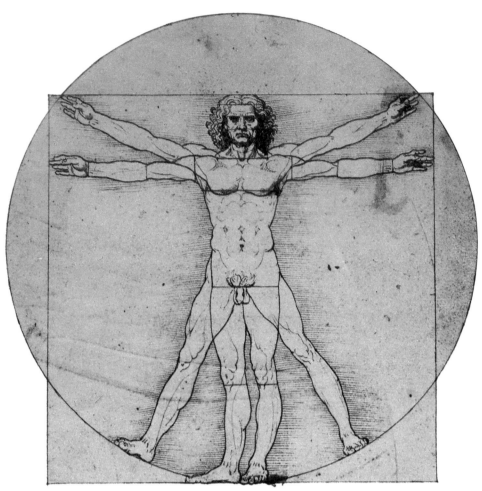

• • •

SQUARE CHAMBER
AND CIRCULAR DOME

• • •

In investigating ancient versions of universal structure, it is characteristic that the two geometrical shapes which predominate are the square and the circle. It is through the reconciliation of these two primary shapes that the essence of sacred architecture emerges.

The square does not exist in nature, it is created by the human mind – dreamed and constructed by us. The circle is god-like, and indicative of wholeness. The symbolic relationship between square and circle is that of human and divine, physical world and spiritual world, imperfect and perfect, qualities. The integration of square and circle is a metaphor for equilibrium between earth and heaven.

The square depicts four cardinal directions in material space on its periphery, while the circle focuses upon its timeless centre. Man has been represented astride both the square and the circle, as shown in Figure 45.

The early 'chamber' type universe depicts the earth as a mountain, the base of which floats upon the ocean; beyond is a high range of mountains which form walls bounding the enclosure of the earthly plane; the ceiling is either domed or vaulted and rests on the walls at strategic points, or is a flat slab suspended above the earth's surface. The firmament is sometimes supported by the world mountain. The heavens are the floor of the celestial realm above, and humanity is understood as having descended from the intersection of heaven and earth.

In early cultures, after megalithic times, the place of prayer was a small cube with a hemispheric cupola above. Whatever the religion, the form is the same. One can still see such buildings all over the Mediterranean; in Greece and Turkey, Egypt and Italy, and across Eastern Europe and Central Asia. The temple or *temenos* is a protected place, circumscribed and separated from the mundane world by augurs, a microcosm of the world as it was pictured in those times – depicting the cubic world and hemispherical heaven. The word *templum* means 'place from which stellar observations are made'.[17] It is also related to the Hebrew word *tabernacle*, which means a tent.

In early Christian cosmology the universe was likened to a chamber, a cubic box with the a lid of the heavens surmounting it. Either the entire box was seen to revolve, or just the lid. The centre of revolution was the constellation of the Great Bear, which was worshipped for its stability. Instead of moving like the other constellations, it appears to simply rotate. To this day the followers of Alice Bailey's science of the Seven Rays invoke the seven stars of the Great Bear when making their invocation.

The heavens were made of either metal or crystal, with holes to allow the celestial light to penetrate. The planets rose through an eastern hole, traversed the sky, and disappeared through a corresponding western hole, only to return after passing through the subterranean world beneath.

Figure 46 • BELOW
Chapel at Palaiochora, Greece. The simple dome surmounts a rectangular solid apse in this typical Greek chapel.

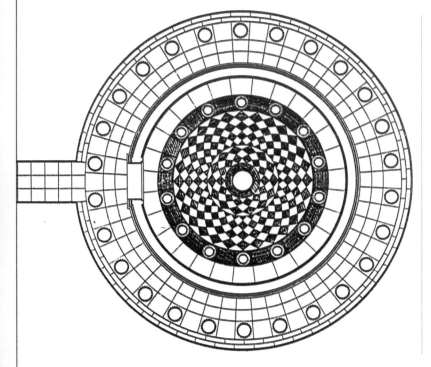

• • •

THE SANCTUARY OF
ASKLEPIOS AT EPIDAURUS

• • •

The site of the fourth century BC sanctuary of the healing god Asklepios at Epidaurus, Greece, is composed of square, circular and semicircular buildings. The Temple of Asklepios is a notable monument of antiquity, a classic of the Doric order, but it is the buildings devoted to healing which strike the eye and soul.

In the original temple was the gold and ivory larger-than-life statue of the god, with one hand on the head of the Divine Snake and the other upon the Sacred Dog. Symbolically the snake is an image of the power of time, which is the creator of disease and the arch-enemy of healing and health. In contrast, the dog is often

FIGURE 47 • ABOVE
Tholos Temple in the Sanctuary of Asklepios at Epidaurus, Greece (c.350 BC). Beneath the circular plan of the Tholos temple is a circular maze, which scholars have speculated was used with snakes for ceremonial purposes

FIGURE 48 • RIGHT
Tholos Temple, Epidaurus, Greece. The walls of the circular maze may be seen in the remains of the Tholos.

associated with the underworld (for example, as Cerberus) and with the Dog Star (Sirius), worshipped by the Egyptians and prominent in all cultures with astronomical mythologies, including classical Greece.

The *Abaton* occupied the entire north side of the temple and was a long, narrow colonnade open on one side to the wonderful view. The healing philosophy of the sanctuary was that everyone, regardless of their infirmity or wealth, had to walk the many kilometres from the port of Epidaurus to the sanctuary, and once there had to spend their first night in the Abaton. They were bathed in the sacred well as part of the required purification of body and soul, and then were given meditations and possibly drugs by the priests before they slept there for the night. When they awoke, the dreams they had had during the night were interpreted by the priests and became the guiding light of the cure. This process has been rediscovered by humanity in this century and is only now being accepted.

The Theatre at Epidaurus was famous throughout the ancient world as the best proportioned and most elegant, as well as for its fantastic acoustics. A whisper on stage could be heard by the more than 12,000 members of the audience, and every seat commanded a perfect view of the entire stage below. It differed from most theatres because its orchestra was circular, and in the centre was an altar. The theatre has been maintained in very good condition and is still being used for performance to this day.

The most interesting and enigmatic building at Epidaurus is the *Tholos*. This round building contains two rings of columns. Beneath the floor are three concentric ringed spaces formed of

monolithic blocks of porous stone. The passages from one circle to the other make it appear like a labyrinth. Similar to the Cretan Labyrinth of Daedalus, it represented the journey of the initiate through the tribulations of life to the still point in the centre. In order to move from one circle to the adjacent one it is necessary to traverse the entire circuit each time. One of the theories offered for its purpose is that it used to house snakes which were sacred to Asklepios, in which case the entire building would have been a symbol of the process of time.

The juxtaposition of square and circle permeates all the ancient mythologies, their pictorial representation, and the early architecture which emerges from the attempt to re-create the universal structure on earth. The process of representing a mythological concept in architectural or pictorial form is a common motif explored in this book.

FIGURE 44 • ABOVE
Dome of the Kaisariani Monastery, Mt Hymettus, Greece. The motif of circular dome and square building is common in the Mediterranean.

FIGURE 50 • RIGHT
Teepees on the shore of Two Medicine Lake, Glacier National Park, Montana, USA. The circular tent of the native American is a reflection of the dome of the sky.

• • •

THE NATIVE AMERICAN DIVINE TENTPOLE

• • •

While many circular forms in architecture derive from the hemispherical image of heaven brought down to earth, the tentpole remains a central symbol of the universal core as a reverberation of the polar axis.

Native American medicine lodges had twenty-eight poles radiating from a central pole, an *omphalos* or centre of the world. The number of poles relates to the days in the lunar month and aligns with important star orientations. A central post was placed by the Medicine Man and intersected by the four sacred paths, which converged at the pole. Ceremonial pipes were smoked to celebrate the finding of the centre again, and other rituals utilizing the lodge reflected cosmic movements and were carried out as aspects of the creation.

The entrance to the lodge was to the east, the direction from which the sun enters the world. The building and taking down of the lodge reflected the creation and destruction of the world.

The remains of the *kiva* or meeting place at Aztec Ruins in New Mexico show it to be based upon a similar creation ritual with zodiacal connotations. The *kiva* appears from a distance as a mound in the desert punctuated by regularly spaced openings. It echoes the sacred mountain at the centre of the universe and is also a burial mound signifying the place of interment and rebirth.

The plan, as shown in Figure 51, shows that at the eastern and western ends were slightly larger openings which determined where the medicine man entered. Around the periphery between these two small rooms were six cubicles on each side of the circular *kiva*. Each room was a space of transition for the members of the tribe's animal totems. They would enter through their appropriate archway and dress in the correct ceremonial costumes, before mounting the steps and descending into the circular sunken Chamber of the Sun.

Four columns surrounded the symbolic burial cask and the ritual fire. The smoke from the fire rose through a circular hole in the roof, which was also the entrance for the primary medicine man and the sacrificial victim. As their ceremonies were a reactivation of the sacrifice and rebirth of the sun god, the chamber would have been bathed with the sun's light passing around the space during the day, and stars would have been visible during the night. It was thus a kind of observatory as well as a ritual chamber reflecting the underworld. The twelve totems were their zodiac, and upon the completion of the ceremony, each tribe member would exit through his appropriate cubicle.

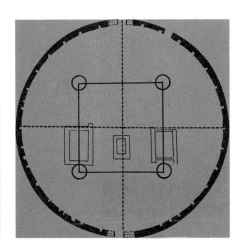

FIGURE 51 • LEFT
Casa Rinconada Plan. The kiva is a circular ceremonial space with four columns supporting the roof.

FIGURE 52 • BELOW
Mandan Indian O-Kee-Pa Ceremony within the Medi-cine Lodge. A painting by George Catlin (1794-1872) shows the cubic structure of logs supporting the roof, the central fire and the hole above through which the spirits could descend.

FIGURE 53 • ABOVE
*Arched Tomb of Pharaoh
Seti I, Abydos, Egypt
(c.1300 BC). This arched
tomb in the Valley of the
Kings is painted like the sky
and represents the body of the
goddess Nut. The decanates
are shown on the left side
and the zodiac constellations
on the right side.*

• • •

MYTH LEADING TO FORM

• • •

A primary example of the power of myth
is the image of the Egyptian sky goddess
Nut (Night). She is represented on
countless temples and in the sacred
literature of the Egyptian Book of the
Dead. Her body is the arched sky, across
which the sun god and the moon goddess
pass, and she is shown both as a place for
stars and, as a wavy field, as the waters of
heaven. Her image is represented in many
ways within tombs, on the exterior and
lid of the tomb itself, on walls with square
surfaces and arched profiles of the
Pharaoh Seti I, or spread across the
barrel-vaulted ceilings.

In Egyptian mythology, the mythical
king and vegetation god Osiris was killed
and cut into fourteen pieces (months of
the year) by his brother Set (or Typhon),
who took over dominion of all Egypt.
His wife Isis, the goddess of grain, found

all the parts but one and named cities
after them: the head is at Abydos, an ear
at Sais, the left leg at Philas, and so forth.
When Osiris returned (from the underworld) he trained his son Horus to war
with Set and take revenge, which he did
in due course. After his victory Osiris
became god of the underworld.

The myth has both natural and astronomical implications. The earth is Isis,
the Nile Osiris, the sun and air Horus,
and Set is the power of time and
drought.[18] Sirius is the star of Isis, and the
Egyptians also associated the sign Leo
with her because the Nile overflowed
when the sun entered Leo. Osiris was
associated with waters and the entire
yearly cycle (he required 365 offering
tables at his temples), the opposite sign

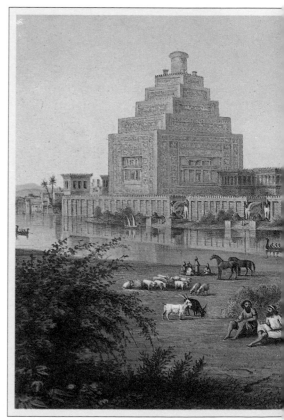

Aquarius, and his tomb was often a hillock, surmounted by a tree. Set corresponded to the principle of dryness and also of the destructive forces of time, breaking down the year into pieces, only to have them recovered every spring by the sun god Horus.

A parallel was established between the sun's movements across the sky and the passage of the dead ferried over the waters of infinity which surrounded the earth. The world of the dead was therefore likened to the geographical boundary of the known world of earth, reproduced within the temple.

The planets and sun floated on the cosmic ocean and moved in their patterns across the ocean-sky in regular motions. Nut was the celestial ocean across which

these planetary movements took place. The sun was special because during the day, the stars which constituted Nut's body were hidden. The sun and stars existed in two different domains of the sacred, separated by the boundary of the horizon. Ancient cultures worshipped these intersections between day and night as celestial creation points and also as boundaries of their known universe. What happened beyond, under or over this vaulted void of being was mysterious, only accessible to the gods.

Nut's body was the brilliant blue of the clear night sky, and the stars were her flesh and blood. The universe was the 'Great Dwelling' to the Egyptians. Set had dominance over the hall of the earth, while Nut reigned over the hall of the

FIGURE 54 • BELOW
Reconstruction of the Palace of Nimrud (9th-8th centuries BC). This reconstruction of the Palace of Nimrud (by J. Ferguson) shows the sophistication of the Chaldeans. The stepped pyramid to the left may have been used for astronomical observations.

heaven, and she is also shown inside mummy cases.[19]

Different beliefs about the creation of the world yielded views about its construction and form. The terms and process of construction of the universe forms some of the most evocative and powerful poetry of the Hindu Vedas. The Hindus perceived the sun as the measurer of the universe, dividing day from night and also the earthly from the heavenly realms. The division by light is a recurring motif in all early cosmology and sacred architecture.

Sometimes the earth was seen as a vessel afloat on the waters, a bark with a domed ceiling spread around it like a curtain. The Greeks used a circular and convex shield to describe the form of the earth. They often wrote of the dome of the heavens in poetic terms, with Olympus, the home of the gods, being the upper reaches of the dome reflecting the earthly Mount Olympus below. Theophrastus likened the Milky Way to the juncture of the two halves of the

dome that were badly joined, although one wonders how he had the effrontery to question the supreme craftsmanship of the gods!

The proportions of earth and heaven were critical issues in ancient times. It was thought that the earth was twice as long as it was wide. This double square remained a model for the proportion of earth well into medieval times.

* * *

THE HEAVENLY SPHERES

* * *

The Chaldeans were the first to extend the metaphor of a spherical heaven to include the lower world. They saw the sky revolve around the polar axis, and the planets cross in front of the backdrop of stars. They accepted the planets, from the moon with its 29-day lunation cycle to Saturn with its 29½-year cycle. The Chaldean astronomer-astrologers assigned a sphere to each of the seven planetary bodies which they saw as existing within the sphere of the fixed stars like the skins of an onion. Each sphere revolved at its own rate, determined by its distance from the centre. This logic also postulated seven spheres below the earth representing the seven regions of the underworld, through which the soul passed at death before rebirth into the upper realm. The divine astrologers were the keepers of the cosmology, calendar, mysticism and magical arts of the society.

The Pythagorean model was based on the Chaldean model, with the addition of the three spheres of fire, water and air. Each sphere was signified by tones creating a 'music of the spheres'. They also designated spirits for each sphere, and the later Christians and Moslems identified angels with these sacred areas.

FIGURE 55 • BELOW
Babylon. This reconstruction shows a square plan with a river through the centre of the city. A spiral tower is the most prominent building, which may be an observatory.

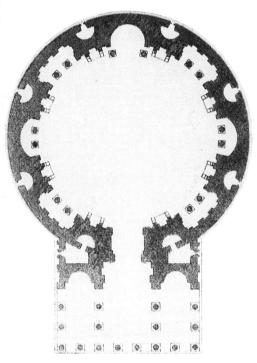

The spherical model of creation spread to virtually all early cultures and became central to their iconography and their architecture. The spheres of the Hindu universe surrounded Mount Meru. The spherical quality of heaven was reconciled with the flatness of earth – because of the great distances, earth represented flatness as heaven did sphericality.

The Pantheon in Rome exactly contains a sphere. The distance from the floor to the apex of the dome (43.5m) equals the diameter of the dome. The dome has a single aperture 9.1m across, through which the sun's rays sweep across the temple floor and through which stars may be seen at night. It has an octagonal geometry; the main entrance occupies one niche, and the gods and goddesses of the seven planets occupy the other seven.

Even as late as the Renaissance, philosophers such as Robert Fludd

illustrated their schemes of cosmic structure with circular spheres representing the various levels of being in the universe, as well as its structure and creation.

The cosmic spheres were associated with angels or *devas*, the motivating forces

FIGURE 56 • ABOVE
Frontispiece, Second Book of the Supernatural *by Robert Fludd. This diagram in a book by Robert Fludd shows the planetary levels of being within the human, as well as the spheres of angels, archangels, etc. which lie beyond the human domain in the spiritual realm.*

FIGURE 57 • LEFT
The Pantheon, Rome (c.118-125 AD). The Pantheon is organized by the circle, both in plan and elevation. The distance from the floor to the ceiling is equal to the diameter of the dome. The seven interior niches are dedicated to the planets, while the eighth is the entrance.

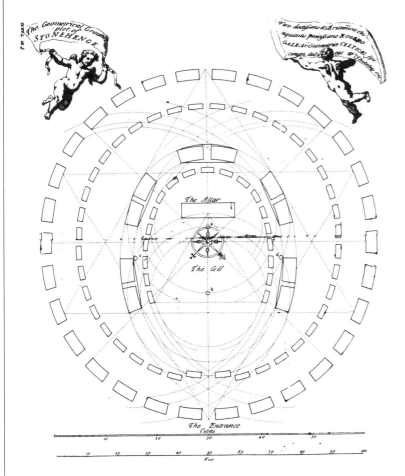

heavens being seen as storeys of a cosmic temple created from pearls, jacinth, gold and silver. Paradise is the seventh heaven. Each heaven is separated from those adjacent by veils and thrones symbolize the powers of each level.

In Norse mythology, the Yggdrasil world ash tree was surrounded by a crystalline sphere through which the stars and planets shone.

The early Christian fathers used the *tabernacle*, to describe creation and the structure of the universe. The symbolism of the tabernacle was inherited from Semitic religions. The 'house of God' is a travelling trunk with a rounded lid, similar in form to the Egyptian tombs featuring paintings of the sky goddess Nut. The tabernacle of Moses enclosed the sun, the stars and the heavens surmounted by a gigantic double ceiling.

FIGURE 58 • ABOVE
Geometry of Stonehenge. This drawing by William Stukeley in 1723 shows his analysis of the geometry of Stonehenge. One can see the vesica piscis and the circle as primary organizing devices.

FIGURE 59 • RIGHT
Yggdrasil Tree. The Frontispiece to The Heroes of Asgard, *illustrated by Huard, shows the Scandinavian conception of the world with the Yggdrasil ash tree at the core, its roots in Hell and its branches defining the hemisphere of the earthy domain, continuing up into Heaven.*

FIGURE 60 • FAR RIGHT
The Fall of Jericho. The Jewish Tabernacle containing the torah is carried as the horns signal the Fall of Jericho.

behind them. The influence of these spirits could be attracted by recreating their spherical domains, and this may have been a further motivation for creating circular and hemispheric places of worship, from Stonehenge and other early stone circles to the latest synchrocyclotrons under the Alps, created to find the spirits of atomic energy.

The angelic hierarchies were described in ancient texts, and in literature such as Cicero's *Dream of Scipio* and Dante's *Divine Comedy*. The primary organizing factor in the spheres is the seven planets, each shining body imbuing its ring with particular qualities, colours and powers. Use of seven planetary spheres is common to the Egyptians, Chaldeans, Zoroastrians, Hindus, Persians, American Indians, Chinese, early Christians and Arabs.

In the Qur'an the spheres are given a specifically architectural quality, the

It is clear that what we consider early mythologies were originally explanations of the workings of nature. In those times astronomical and astrological concepts were transmitted through myth and religious rites, and encoded into calendars. The gods were creators, and their homes were the sacred places on earth which reflected those in heaven. The world was a mysterious symbol and carried immense power because of this.

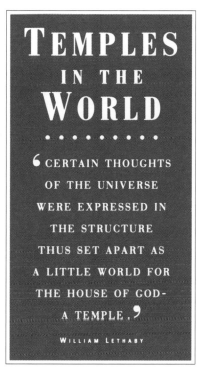

TEMPLES IN THE WORLD

• • • • • • • • •

❝ CERTAIN THOUGHTS OF THE UNIVERSE WERE EXPRESSED IN THE STRUCTURE THUS SET APART AS A LITTLE WORLD FOR THE HOUSE OF GOD - A TEMPLE. ❞

WILLIAM LETHABY

The simplicity of primeval life was easily related to this cosmic symbolism for the yearly round of seasons which governed life in the fields and hearth, the sowing and reaping of crops, and the raising of livestock, paralleled the movements of the sun, moon, planets and other celestial bodies through the skies. The realms of the earth mother and the gods of the underworld were deep within the ground in caves or mounds, and the oceans that bound the entire physical world had their heavenly equivalent in the sky.

The first temples were trees ceremonially decorated with symbols of the gods within the fields of stars above, and early temple architecture reflected the glory of these simple places. Both the sky and the surrounding oceans were obviously circular, and the temples reflected this circularity. As Lethaby stated:

WHEN THE WORLD WAS A TREE, EVERY TREE WAS IN SOME SORT ITS REPRESENTATION; WHEN A TENT OR A BUILDING, EVERY TENT OR BUILDING; BUT WHEN THE RELATION WAS FIRMLY ESTABLISHED, THERE WAS ACTION AND REACTION BETWEEN THE SYMBOL AND THE REALITY, AND IDEAS TAKEN FROM ONE WERE TRANSFERRED TO THE OTHER, UNTIL THE SYMBOLISM BECAME COMPLICATED, AND ONLY PARTICULAR BUILDINGS WOULD BE SELECTED FOR THE SYMBOLIC PURPOSE; CERTAIN FORMS WERE REASONED FROM THE BUILDING TO THE WORLD, AND CONVERSELY CERTAIN THOUGHTS OF THE UNIVERSE WERE EXPRESSED IN THE STRUCTURE THUS SET APART AS A LITTLE WORLD FOR THE HOUSE OF GOD - A TEMPLE.[20]

For the Teutons, who worshipped the tree as the universal temple, temple and tree were interchangeable words. The figures painted on cave walls and decorating the earliest temples were not only representations of sacred animals or

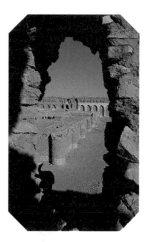

FIGURE 61 • FAR LEFT
Monastery on Mount Athos, Greece. Monasteries were often built in mountainous places which shared the sacred qualities of the 'world mountain'.

FIGURE 62 • ABOVE
Al Ukheidhir, Iraq. The archway reflects the cave entrances from which humanity ascended.

FIGURE 63 • BELOW
Great Stupa and East Gate at Sanchi, India. The circles at the apex of the mountain indicate higher levels of being.

celestial beings, but were an embodiment of them as well. The legendary temples of Babylon contained images of the luminaries, representations of the celestial spheres, and statues of the cosmic beings which created the world. The planetary symbolism was prevalent and primary.

The Hindu and Buddhist conception of the universe is as a vast ocean upon which the world floats. From the holy mountain at the centre terraces descend, with humanity occupying the lowest level, guardian deities the middle tiers, and the heavens the top. Most architectural forms reflected this organization. The belief that the gods also lived in mountain caves gave rise to the mound

and womb architecture. Some temples, such as those at Ajanta and Ellora, were carved out of mountains, complete with barrel vaults, tracery around windows and representations of carved timber throughout. All Hindu temples are mountains, as are Buddhist *stupas*. Both were originally mounds of earth, eventually faced with stone or brick for permanence. These buildings mark sacred places, where reliquaries were discovered or kept, or places where the gods, the Buddha or their followers presided.

The Emperors of China during the Chan dynasty held court in the Hall of Light which was a perfect cube surmounted by a dome.

FIGURE 64 • BELOW
Ellora Caves, India (7th-8th centuries AD). Magnificent temples were carved out of the rock at Ellora, reinforcing the sacredness of the cave.

FIGURE 65 • LEFT
East Gate of the Main Stupa at Sanchi, India (1st century BC) The world tree is a primary motif on these gates leading to the stupa as world mountain.

FIGURE 66 • RIGHT
*Sanganer Jain Temple, India.
Temple images are a reminder
of the gods residing there.*

• • •

THE HINDU COSMIC TEMPLE

• • •

Hindu temples contain the *shakti* or Divine Spirit, which is a present entity or force flowing through the forms in a determined way. This explains the Hindu's interest in the laws governing the activation of architecture.

The symbolism of the temples is similar. The pinnacle of the dome is surmounted by umbrellas, symbolizing the passage of the soul through the layers of consciousness; the four gates are aligned with the cardinal points and marked with the wheel, tree, trident and lotus; and the clockwise walkways describe circular devotions around the shrine. Some were even personified by having eyes looking in all directions, gazing at the world through hooded lids.

The Hindus integrate the concept of the temple with astronomical and astrological symbols.[21] Once the orientation has been determined by the sun, the internal arrangement of the building is decided by a set pattern. A mandala form describes each of the required temple plans. The squares correspond to major and minor functions of the temple, with the central square being symbolically situated outside the cosmic order as the place where Brahma dwells. Over this a cube is erected symbolizing the divinity.

There are thirty-two types of mandala governing temples, divided into two groups. Those derived from the basic mandala of nine squares symbolize earth, with the central square as the centre of the world, and the remaining eight being the cardinal points and intermediate regions of space. Those derived from the fourfold, quaternary mandala are symbolic of Shiva as transformer expressing the principle of Time. This wheel has no spokes, just an intersection of squares which exists in present time.

As Burckhardt notes, the favoured plans use squares divided into either sixty-four or eighty-one lesser squares, an interesting combination because both are multiples of the length of the precessional Great Year (64 x 81 x 5 lunar-solar years = 25,920 years).[22] The temple is therefore an abstraction of the universe, and a sum of all cosmic cycles. The central squares of either four or nine components are the 'embryo chambers'.

The eight directions of space are associated with the seven planets plus the demon of the eclipses, Rahu. The squares around the edge of the *Bramasthana* denote the twelve solar divinities. In a sixty-four square mandala the border represents the twenty-eight lunar mansions, and in the eighty-one square mandala four guardians of the cardinal regions are combined with the mansions (28 + 4). In overall format, one defines the cross by central lines and the other by rows of squares.

The object of the orientation is to fix and locate the temple in time and space, in relation to the sun and moon. Similarly the Hindu and Buddhist fixation with statuary representing male and female mating reflects the dance of the cosmic rhythms into a single timeless whole. The Hindus also designed entire celestial cities based on the same geometries. In the domain of Christian iconography the Heavenly Jerusalem is a primary goal and prototype of the Christian temple.

The orientation and plan of temples often express both a cosmology and an astrology, crystallizing a thought form in time and space, and transforming the mundane into the cosmic and godlike. The Chinese Hall of Distinction[23] possessed a structure which reflected the solar ritual required by the Emperor. It was divided into nine squares and the ritual involved passing from room to room as the sun passed from mansion (sign) to mansion. Each room contained its correct dress, colours and symbolism.

The Aztecs of Tenochtitlán worshipped the Pleiades, which played a central role in their religion and its complex calendar based upon the idea of cyclical time. For the Aztecs the world ended at the culmination of a fifty-two-year cycle (a 'bundling of the years' of four groups of thirteen years), at which they performed a New Fire Ceremony on top of Cerro de la Estrella, the 'Hill of the Star'. From the astronomically oriented temple built on the apex of the hill the priests watched as the Pleiades passed the zenith, signalling the salvation of the world, after which a human victim was sacrificed and another cycle began.[24]

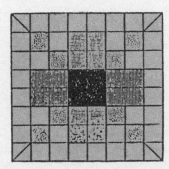 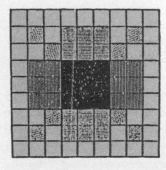

FIGURE 67 • LEFT
Vastu-Purusha Temple Mandalas. The mandala of 64 divisions on the left symbolizes the principle of time, while the mandala of 81 divisions on the right symbolizes earth.

• • •

THE HERMETIC TEMPLE

• • •

A new definition of temple emerged as a result of the Hermetic tradition.[25] The major temples express and preserve a sacred canon of measurement embodied in the native laws, customs, legends, symbols, architecture and rituals. The temple was a model cosmology and integral to the psychic coherence of an entire culture.[26]

The temple was considered a living organism whose physical body was a reflection of the body of the gods, the solar system. A standard for inner and outer organization was initiated in the temple, and spread outward to government and social institutions at every level. As in Chinese acupuncture the human body is criss-crossed with energy channels called meridians, and acupuncture needles are placed to activate points along these meridians, so on the body of earth the temples activated sacred places and served as a conduit of cosmic, spiritual energy.

The Hebrew temple contained an omphalos, the Stone of Foundation, a symbolic replica of the first created thing of the earth, and the embryo from which the temple itself was born into the world. The temple was a sacred centre for reconciliation and integration, just as it combined mathematics, cosmology, spiritual initiation and beauty.

FIGURE 68 • ABOVE
Barfreston Church, Kent, England (c.1180). The figure of Christ appears in the vesica piscis within the hemicircular entrance of Barfreston Church.

After the destruction of the original Temple of Jerusalem the early Christians recreated its symbolism in the 'New Jerusalem', an anticipated return of the ancient wisdom and an inspiration for prophecy. The New Jerusalem contained mathematical formulae which symbolized the potential integration of the world. St Augustine's *City of God* is a hermetic, numerological and symbolist work which extends this metaphor to include the world. We aspire to create a New World through the New Jerusalem.

John Michell's model of the New Jerusalem is developed from a diagram of terrestrial and lunar spheres (see Figure 69) and is measured in feet instead of miles. Around one circle of the earth are placed twelve circles corresponding to the size of the moon, arranged in groups like the zodiac, so that the circumference of each of the two outer circles touches the point where the circle drawn through their centres meets the square of equal perimeter. The circles are inscribed within a twelve-sided figure.

This geometric reconstruction of the New Jerusalem corresponds to St John's description of the Holy City as having twelve gates, three in each cardinal direction, a foursquare shape, and a peripheral measurement of twelve thousand furlongs. In the centre of the city is the tree of life, bearing all manner of fruits, yielding her fruit each month, and with leaves that will heal the nations. The twelve pearls at the gates and the fruits of the tree of life correspond to the twelve lunar circles around the periphery, because 2,160 miles is the diameter of the moon and 2,160 years the length of the Platonic month, the time it takes the sun to move through one complete precessional sign. The twelve circles

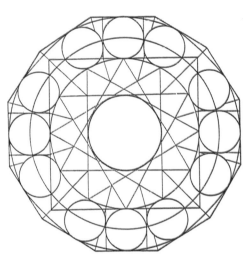

represent the twelve signs, and the whole is both an image of the universe and a model of time, containing astronomical distances and astrological times.[27]

This example of astronomy, geometry and astrology meeting in a city or building plan, albeit an imaginary one, shows the intention of the Hermetic mysteries as they apply to sacred architecture.

FIGURE 69 • ABOVE
*The New Jerusalem.
John Michell's geometric
reconstruction of the New
Jerusalem is based on a circle
the size of the earth
surrounded by 12 circles the
size of the moon, all
inscribed within a
12-sided figure.*

FIGURE 70 • LEFT
*Winchester Round Table.
The Arthurian Round Table
mounted on a wall in
Winchester was both a sacred
place and a symbol of
knightly equality under God.
The 24 black and white
places seem like positive and
negative expressions of the
twelve zodiac signs.*

THE DOMAIN OF THE SACRED

I t is essential to understand the way in which sacred sites are located because this is one of the basic principles of sacred architecture. Early sacred sites invariably occupied what people recognized as special habitations of the gods on earth. In ancient cultures such as those of Greece, India, Japan, Africa, Australia and the Americas, islands, mountains, seas, waterways, and trees were given sacred characteristics.

> ❝ YOU CLIMB THE MOUNTAINS SURVEYING THE EARTH, YOU SUSPEND FROM THE HEAVENS THE CIRCLE OF THE LANDS. ❞
>
> THE GREAT HYMN TO SHAMASH, BABYLONIAN CREATOR GOD

which determined appropriate places for living and for worshipping the gods.

The most natural location was near a spring or well. Sacred springs and wells were considered places of increased fertility, for curing illness, for encouraging prophecy and for addressing the spiritual. The energy of such places is fresh and pure, and the proximity of natural water was used and sanctified by megalithic man, by the Druids, Romans and

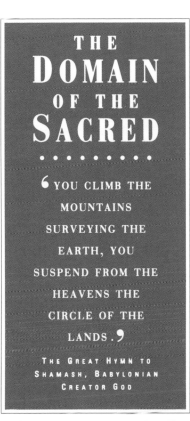

FIGURE 71 • FAR LEFT *Father of Psyche sacrificing to Apollo. In the painting by Claude Lorrain (1600-82) a sacrifice is made in the midst of a sacred natural site.*

FIGURE 72 • BELOW LEFT *Chalice Well, Glastonbury, Somerset, England. The Chalice Well was a sacred natural place from the earliest times. Its cover is decorated with the vesica piscis.*

FIGURE 73 • BELOW *Castalia Fountain Cave, Delphi, Greece. The Temple of Apollo at Delphi was originally located in a cave in the mountain side by the source of the Castalian fountain.*

• • •

NATURAL SACRED CENTRES

• • •

While humanity has always marked out certain places in which to worship their gods, there are principles which determine the foundation of the sacred which we of the modern era have lost sight of. In humanity's prehistory there were needs

FIGURE 74 • ABOVE

Coronation Chair and Stone of Destiny,
Westminster Abbey, London. All the kings
and queens of England have been crowned
above the 'Stone of Destiny' in Westminster
Abbey. The stone, guarded by four lions, is
directly beneath the seat of the chair.

Christians. Not only was water considered to be a necessity at sacred sites, its importance is also reflected in its use in baptism and other sacred rituals.

Many waters have been known for their therapeutic qualities. The well at Glastonbury has a high iron content, and such chalybeate (iron-bearing) springs have curative properties, around which religious establishments have been created.

Single stones and outcroppings also mark sacred places. It was considered that earth spirits inhabited such stones. Kings and Queens of England are enthroned above the Stone of Destiny in Westminster Abbey and Apollonian priestesses consulted the spirits of prophecy of the God at the Omphalos at Delphi. The Ka'aba at Mecca is believed to have fallen from heaven to earth, and as a result carries heavenly energies to man.

The *omphalos* (navel) at Delphi was sited strategically at what the Greeks considered the centre of the world, although there were other omphalos sites throughout Greece and Egypt which often marked oracular centres.[28] According to Greek legends, Deukalion's (Noah's) Ark landed on Mount Parnassus above Delphi and he threw his mother Gaia's bones behind to repopulate the earth. Another myth is that Zeus sent two swans to find the earth's true centre and their paths crossed at Delphi, defining the location of the omphalos. Some representations of omphalos stones have crossed swan designs. The stone marked the centre and was a focus of earth energies which had previously been dispersed throughout the land at random, as the shrine of the earth goddess Gaia.

The basket-like pattern around the *omphalos* at Delphi (see Figure 76) is a

geodetic mesh which indicates that it and other omphalos stones mark specific locations on the planet, including one at the temple of Ammon at Thebes[29] in Egypt. These critical locations signify a level of understanding of geodetic matters which far surpasses that believed to have been known in ancient times. The serpent images associated with Delphi, and the oracular centre dedicated to Apollo there, also represent the taming of the serpent power of time and space, fixing it at a sacred place and harnessing its positive qualities.

The cosmic struggle to contain this evocation of what the Chinese call the dragon power is also reflected in the legends of St George, Beowulf, St Michael and other saints and heroes.

FIGURE 75 • ABOVE
Serpent Symbols, Temple of Sobek, Kom Ombo, Egypt. The serpents represent the power of time and space, and their use on temples or head-dresses shows these powers harnessed in a sacred act.

FIGURE 76 • LEFT
Omphalos, Delphi, Greece. The omphalos was found by Apollo as the tomb symbol for Python, and subsequently became a cult object and symbol of the centre of the world. The basket-like pattern enwrapping the stone consists of geodetic lines showing the location of sacred cult places around the Mediterranean.

Enediat to   uerbum cuis ad audienda
nunium os   uacem sermonum cuis p3.
angeli cuis   Enedicanima mea do
potentes uirtute qui faaas mino et omma que mtra

The Ka'aba at Mecca contains a magnetic stone which fell from the sky and is the most holy shrine of Islam. It is surrounded by a black cube and is the focus of all Islamic prayers. The siting of all Islamic holy buildings and monuments take the location of Mecca into consideration, and the development of Arabic astronomy owed much to this requirement. In this case practical needs governed metaphysical considerations in the process of making astronomy and the sacred in architecture a unified whole.

Hills such as Mount Ararat in Turkey, Glastonbury Tor in Somerset, Avebury Hill in Wiltshire or St Michael's Mount in Cornwall are holy hills which act as a focus of spiritual energies. Similarly, later monuments such as the pyramids of Egypt, Central and South America, and

FIGURE 77 • ABOVE
St Michael Slaying the Dragon. The painting in the Tres Riches Heures du Duc de Berry, *by Pol Limbourg shows St Michael slaying the dragon against the backdrop of Mont St Michel in France. It was known in pagan times as Dinsul, the holy Mount of the Sun. The theme of defeating the nemesis of time and space is the ultimate cosmic struggle.*

FIGURE 78 • RIGHT
Mt Ararat, Turkey. Mt Ararat is believed to be where Noah's Ark landed and has been a sacred mountain since ancient times.

FIGURE 79 • LEFT
Mount Fuji and Lake Yananaka, Japan. Mount Fuji is a potent sacred symbol for the Japanese.

FIGURE 80 • BOTTOM
Glastonbury Tor, Somerset. The sides of the pre-Christian Glastonbury Tor were modelled into a vast three-dimensional labyrinth. This was the holy hill of the Celtic god of the underworld, Gwyn ap Nudd.

religious buildings and complexes in south-eastern Asia are all man-made representations of holy mountains.

Smaller representations of the sacred mountain exist as burial mounds which proliferated in all areas in prehistory. In Neolithic times sacred sites were claimed from nature and eventually became prototypes of the earliest monuments such as burial mounds. Between 5000 and 2000 BC the New Stone Age people built many monuments across Europe, both burial mounds and rings of standing stones. In recent years astronomers have discovered that both the mounds and the rings have astronomical significance, both in their siting and in their form.

• • •
IRISH MEGALITHIC MAGIC
• • •

Between 3700 and 3200 BC the Neolithic inhabitants of Ireland built imposing stone structures along the meandering Boyne river amidst a landscape already dotted with mounds, standing stones and earthworks. What makes Newgrange, Knowth and Dowth special, apart from the fact that they are among the oldest known remaining human buildings, is that they are solar observatories built to a tolerance and understanding thought to be unknown until millennia later.

The abstract art of the great number of carved stone engravings in and around the monuments hint at a greater mystery. These mounds contain long passages aligned in such a way that the sun shines into the central chamber of the mound at particular times of the year. According to archaeologists the explosion of light at specific days was merely a side-effect of what were really just burial mounds, and the strange spiralling carvings outside and inside were merely decorations.

In fact the mounds were accurate chronometers of the sun and there was a clear link between the monuments and the Neolithic art of the builders.[30] Supportive evidence of the tradition of such architecture exists in the poetry and literature of Irish mythology. The Irish knew the earliest native gods to be a 'supernatural race of wizards and magicians'[31] who descended from the sky before the Celts. These 'Lords of Light' dwelt in a timeless realm of mystery at Newgrange, and its sacred qualities shone forth over the isle. The River Boyne flowed from the underworld of the well of Segais, the source of all wisdom and occult knowledge, and its waters carried mystic aspirations in every bubbling drop.

Newgrange was the home of the Irish god of wisdom Dagda, who was also the god of the sun. His son was magically conceived and born at Newgrange during a lengthening of the day. To this day the mounds are considered not merely as burial mounds, but also as homes of the living gods. Although it was not adopted

FIGURE 81 • ABOVE
Boyne Valley, Co. Meath, Ireland. The River Boyne sweeps majestically through the Irish countryside and some of the most powerful megalithic mounds in Europe are found along its course.

FIGURE 82 • RIGHT
Boyne Valley Map. This plan shows the many megalithic sites along the River Boyne. Line A marks the Summer Solstice Sunset, line B marks the Nov/Feb Cross-Quarter Day Sunset, and line C marks the orientation of a minor lunar standstill.

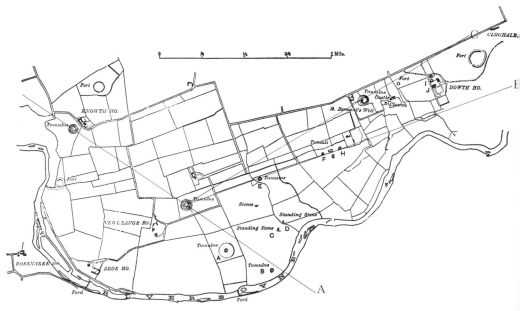

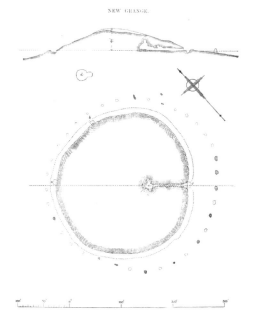

NEW GRANGE.

FIGURE 83 • ABOVE LEFT
*Newgrange, Ireland, Section
and Plan. The passage grave
at Newgrange (c.3000 BC)
was originally surrounded by
a ring of stones, few of which
survive.*

FIGURE 84 • ABOVE
*Newgrange, Detail Section
and Plan of the Chamber.
At the Winter Solstice
(21 December) the rays of the
rising sun enter the chamber
over the stone above the
entrance and penetrate to the
back stone.*

FIGURE 85 • CENTRE
LEFT *This stone basin was
used for ceremonial purposes or
for reflecting light in the
deepest recess of Newgrange.*

FIGURE 86 • CENTRE
RIGHT *The decorations with
symbolic and numerical
significance carved on the
interior stones all describe
astronomical movements.*

FIGURE 87 • LEFT
*Newgrange, Entrance Stone
and 'Roof Box'. The Roof
Box is a special aperture which
allows light from the rising sun
at the Winter Solstice to enter
the passage.*

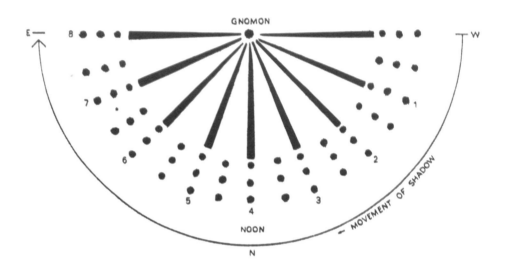

FIGURE 88 • RIGHT
Newgrange, Cairn Sundial Carved on Stone. At many Irish megalithic sites are carvings which provided accurate sundials for determining yearly times.

FIGURE 89 • BOTTOM RIGHT *Newgrange, Spiral Stones. The Irish rock engraving techniques were highly sophisticated. Here is an equable spiral pickmarked on the stone.*

by the later Celts, the symbolism of the sun permeates early Irish mythology.

Newgrange had deteriorated into a featureless mound when its opening was discovered in 1699 by the British General, Charles Vallancey, who also found that it had an astronomical orientation, and called it the 'Cave of the Sun'.[32] The interior contained a cross-shaped passage lined with large flat stones. At the Winter Solstice the sun's rays penetrated all the way into the monument and shone on the back wall almost thirty metres within. Due to the details of the construction the light enters through a roof-box above the doorway.

At Dowth and Knowth are smaller mounds which exhibit similar properties, but are oriented to other phenomena. Knowth receives the sun's rays at the Equinox sunset and strange patterns are cast on two curbstones at the base of the passage mound. It has passages facing both east and west and sundials engraved on nearby stones. The western passage was

built 500 years before Newgrange, and the light beam extends much further into its centre, along a narrower passage. What is intriguing is that at maximum depth the passage veers to the right. This is assumed to be the remains of an earlier, smaller mound, but could be accounted

for by understanding the shift in alignment caused by the precession of the equinoxes.

The most interesting features in the Boyne Valley are the carvings on the stones outside and within these mounds. They were catalogued by Brennan who found that they could be categorized into a number of groups. Some are symbols of the sun and moon ascribed to archetypal images of concentric circles, radiating lines from a central circle or a dot within a circle. Others are crosses within circles, squares or diamonds, or outside circles.

The most unusual of all are the many series of wavy lines and spirals. These have been found to be the paths of the sun's rays projected from sundials onto stones and traced throughout a yearly cycle. This movement forms a double spiral, moving clockwise in summer and counter-clockwise in winter. The wavy lines and half-circles are simultaneously connected with the waxing and waning phases of the moon, the divisions of the moon's cycle into quarters, and the daily phases throughout monthly cycles.

Some carvings show sundials which would have been used to tell the time and date. They are so sophisticated that they tell 'planetary hours' which vary in length from summer to winter, and allow the division of the day into eight or sixteen equal parts.[33]

The entire complex in the Boyne Valley is so beautiful and powerful that its rare integration of nature and cosmology strikes the soul and inspires holy thoughts. The people who built them were obviously preoccupied with measuring time, and their architecture is a powerful statement of their beliefs and culture. The cosmic models of rotating spirals and evocative symbols allow art and architecture to merge with integral cosmic principles in a profound way.

FIGURE 90 • ABOVE
Treasury of Atreus, Greece (c.1300-1250 BC). The construction of this much later tomb or treasury reflects that of the Irish megalithic sites.

FIGURE 91 • BELOW
Knowth Passage Mound, Co. Meath, Ireland. The passage mound at Knowth is the largest in Ireland, covering an acre of hilltop land in the Boyne Valley. Around its periphery are more than 134 kerbstones, more than half of which are engraved with carvings.

Sir Norman Lockyer[34] was a distinguished astronomer who travelled throughout the British Isles measuring prehistoric passage graves, tombs, burial mounds, single standing stones, stone rows and circles. He believed that these monuments had a common significance for their builders. He linked these monuments with the sun worship of these people, and proposed that the siting of the monuments reflected the times of the year when certain festivals were timed by astronomical events, such as the location of sunrise and sunset, moonrise and moonset on special days, such as solstices and equinoxes. The monuments

FIGURE 92 • RIGHT
Sir Joseph Norman Lockyer (c.1836-1920), British Astronomer.

FIGURE 93 • BELOW
Castlerigg Stone Circle, Lake District, England (c.3000 BC). The spectacular setting of a northern stone circle which was investigated by Lockyer.

FIGURE 94 • LEFT
*Avebury Stone Circle,
Wiltshire (c.2600-2300 BC).
A small town has been built
within the massive stone circle
and mound at Avebury.*

FIGURE 95 • BELOW
*Silbury Hill, Wiltshire,
England (c.2700 BC).
Silbury Hill is the largest
man-made monument in
Europe and is a part of the
complex including the
Avebury stone circle.*

would therefore have had a significance that went beyond their apparent function as places of burial or meeting. Lockyer also postulated that such early people had a class of astronomer-priests whose function combined religious ceremony with the siting and building of monuments.

It is assumed that such early cultures had a highly advanced 'megalithic science' which informed their culture, religion and architecture – a point which many scientists dispute. They contend that nowhere else in these cultures is there any evidence of a sophisticated understanding of astronomy or building. And yet the Boyne Valley complex exists.

The greatest difficulty in considering megalithic science is that it came into being in a supposedly pre-literate time, and therefore all assumptions about the skills and rationale are purely speculative, at least from a scientific standpoint. The sites have been meticulously measured and computer-analyzed to find the possible or

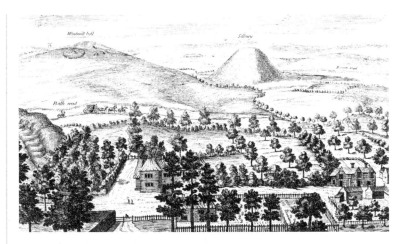

probable astronomical lines which prove their siting. Adverse criticism is based upon the fact that it is impossible to prove that the alignments were anything other than random, although one would have thought the fact that virtually all such sites have significant alignments sways the argument in favour of giving these early people credit for a high level of civilization and technical achievement.

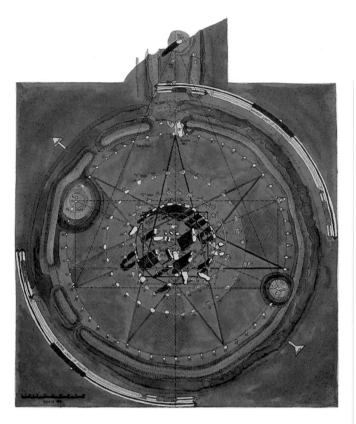

FIGURE 96 • ABOVE
Cosmic Temple of Stone-henge, Wiltshire, England (c.2100-2000 BC). The form of Stonehenge was created by the geometry of the successive rings of stones, the central group being the U-shaped ring of sarsens. The entire monument is oriented as a lunar-solar observatory and calendar.

The area from which the most persuasive proof comes is the mythology and religion of these peoples, which amounted to the same thing. Their fertility and creation myths, their belief in a seasonal cycle, and their views about death and the afterlife which do come down to us seem to support the siting and context of the ancient monuments.

• • •

STONEHENGE

• • •

A primary characteristic of megalithic monuments is their orientation. The rings of stones and burial mounds are all characterized by alignments with celestial objects, from the sun and moon, to the Pole Star Polaris, to Sirius, to lesser planets, and to constellations. Since these objects were considered gods and goddesses and direct representations of the powers which were believed to govern humanity, their influence was paramount.

One of the first discoveries which planted the germ that megalithic cultures had a form of astronomy was Stukeley's recognition that Stonehenge was oriented to the midsummer rising sun. As Stonehenge still remains one of the most powerful and convincing examples of megalithic astronomy and architecture, it is worth studying in detail.

Stonehenge was apparently used for a number of purposes simultaneously - as a sacred ceremonial centre, a priestly observatory, a measuring device for the calculation of accurate calendars, a burial monument, and as a container or transmitter of powerful earth energies. The purposes attributed to it vary according to the bias of those who have studied it, but it seems clear that these many purposes were integral to its functioning.

The overall geometry of Stonehenge is determined by squaring the circle.[35] The outermost circle of sarsen stones determines a square within which the diameter of the bluestone ring can be determined. When a Seal of Solomon is constructed within this circle, the size of the smallest bluestone horseshoe ring is defined.

The circumference of the outer sarsen circle and the square encircling it is equal to 316.8 feet, a symbolic number also describing the measure around the New Jerusalem in miles. John Michell believes that the Holy City of St John's vision, the outlines of which are also found at Glastonbury, precedes Christian revelation and was understood by the builders of Stonehenge. It was a model of the cosmic order created on earth.

A larger scale solar geometry determines the relative sizes of the rings at Stonehenge.[36] A cross drawn through the centre of Stonehenge allows the construction of two vesica pisces at right angles to

FIGURE 97 • LEFT
Stonehenge in Winter.

each other, one enclosing and one enclosed within the sarsen ring. When a vesica is in turn inscribed within the innermost one, the enclosed diamond has an area of 1080 square feet, 1080 being the sacred number of the Holy Ghost. These measurements use the Megalithic Yard (MY), a unit sacred to early humanity. The largest intersecting circles have a total width of 666 MY, a number sacred to the sun. Stonehenge may therefore be seen as a sanctuary to the earth spirit penetrated by the sun's rays.

Stonehenge is thought to have been built over a long period of time, between 1900 and 1600 BC, because the rings of standing stones are made of different materials and clearly were erected at different times. The sarsens average thirty tons each and are from the Marlborough Downs, while the bluestones are from Wales. The sarsen stones in the centre form a horseshoe shape surrounded by a circle of bluestones, which are surrounded by another complete circle of sarsens. A ring of 'Z' holes is surrounded by a ring of 'Y' holes, and then, after a distance, the outermost ring of Aubrey holes. At the same distance from the centre as the Aubrey holes are two mounds and the fallen Slaughter Stone along the Avenue. The entire ensemble is surrounded by a concentric ditch and mound with gaps that occur periodically, and an entrance at the intersection of the Avenue leading to the Heel Stone.

FIGURE 98 • LEFT
Stonehenge at Sunset.

The primary alignment factor is the axis of the avenue leading from the centre of the circle to the Heel Stone, located to the north-east. This orientation allowed the Heel Stone to be used to sight the solstitial sunrise in Megalithic times. The Heel is slightly offset due to the later building of the Avenue and ditch, but provides a warning of some days before the solstice point which could have been used to determine the time of the solstice more exactly. Some regard the Heel Stone as a lunar alignment device as well.

The relative sizes and proportions, and the construction sequence of the stone circles at Stonehenge deserve attention. Stonehenge I, the first part of the monument, was started about 1900 BC. Late

Stone Age people dug a gigantic circular ditch and piled the rubble outside into a pair of banks on each side. The circle was left open to the north-east, where four little holes were dug, probably to hold wooden posts. Two stones were placed upright at the opening and the larger Heel Stone located 100 feet outside the circle. They dug a trench around the Heel Stone and immediately filled it in with chalk. Then they dug the ring of fifty-six Aubrey holes just inside the bank. These holes could have been used to predict eclipses.

At this time Stonehenge was a sacred enclosure defined by the chalk white inner edge of the surrounding ditch. The Heel Stone was also surrounded by a twelve foot diameter circle of white chalk to assert its sacredness. Its simple geometry was defined by a rectangle perpendicular to the Heel Stone axis defined by the four station stones, with the two circular mounds at the diagonals. This 'mystic rectangle' shape has historical, ritualistic, astrological, geometric and astronomical significance.[37] Carbon 14 tests also verify that numerous burials on the site were carried out at this time.

About 1750 BC the Beaker people built the two bluestone circles of which comprise Stonehenge II. The outermost bluestone circle is defined by constructing a septangle within the Aubrey hole circle. The intersections of the legs of the septangle define the diameter of the inner circle.

The building of Stonehenge III by the Bronze Age people consisted primarily of the removal and replacement of the outer bluestone circle with larger sarsen boulders and continuous lintels, and the creation of the horseshoe of five giant trilithon sarsens with lintels in the centre of the circle. The lintels were held in place by a mortise and tenon system of knobs, and these stones are the most impressive part of the modern monument. The central horseshoe was also defined by the septangle's innermost legs.

The sarsen horseshoe defines the sunrise, sunset, moonrise and moonset positions, and completes the astronomical functioning of the entire creation. But the most impressive aspect of the Stonehenge geometry is its ability to measure the nineteen-year Metonic cycle which allows the accurate prediction of eclipses.

An interesting hypothesis presented by Michael Saunders in 1982[38] was that Stonehenge was the first planetarium. Using the measurements of the various rings of stones from the centre of the monument, Saunders discovered that when they are multiplied by 10^{10}, they correspond, to within a few per cent, to the distances of the planets from the Sun to Jupiter. Mercury corresponds to the semi-circular bluestone ring of trilithons; the Sun to the sarsen horseshoe; Venus to the second bluestone ring of fifty-six stones; the Earth to the sarsen ring of thirty uprights; the nearest and furthest possible orbits of Mars correspond to the two Y and Z rings; the asteroids to the surrounding circular bank; and Jupiter to the Heel Stone, with the chalk circle around the stone representing the mean distance of Jupiter's orbit. He also found that the length of the Avenue corresponds to the mean distance of Pluto from the Sun. It is a superb illustration of the way in which the mathematics of this remarkable structure represents an archetype of planetary relationships in symbolic form.

Stonehenge is a solar-lunar observatory and temple, and is the ultimate in such monuments anywhere in the world. Hawkins considers it a very sophisticated computer, making it the first in history. Its siting and geometry integrate it within its environment in such a way that mythology, religion, science and the pursuit of the sacred coincide.

FIGURE 101 • BELOW
Stonehenge at Sunset.

• • •

THE INTERSECTION
OF TIME AND SPACE

• • •

The most common siting device for sacred places is the cross of the four cardinal directions north, south, east and west. The axes of the cardinal directions are important because they unite angles in space, but also in time. Many early monuments and later diagrams are simultaneously pictures of architecture and calendars. This dual meaning is common to many sacred sites.

The Maya of Central America carved designs which showed the cardinal points as intersections of time and space. The designs occur in forty or more locations in Central America, particularly around Teotihuacán, and have a basic similarity of form - that of a cross shape surrounded by concentric circles.[39] Most often the shapes are picked out in dots rather than by a continuous line. The number of dots in each design (often adding up to the lunar number 260 in multiples of thirteen and twenty) link the diagrams with calendrical numbers. In some cases fringes of light seem to emanate from the outer of the concentric circles, which seem to represent the sun and its halo of light. The same design occurs as a game board for *patolli*[40] as well as a design and sacred architecture plan.

The entire monument of Teotihuacán is a reflection of the cross-and-circle design, and its main thoroughfares cross at right angles, and resemble the design. Two huge pyramids, similar in area to the Great Pyramid but half the height, are positioned to strengthen the axes of the avenues. The anomaly of this grand siting example is that the avenues deviate from an alignment with the north-south and east-west axes by more than 15°, yet align perfectly with cross-and-circle designs carved into cliffs and used for siting the city itself. While the builders knew the correct axes, they apparently chose to align the great city with the axes of the rising and setting points of the major constellation known as Pleiades.

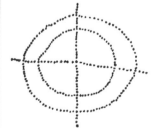

FIGURE 102 • ABOVE
Cross and Circle at Cerrito el Chapin, near Alta Vista, Mexico. These stone carvings show the importance of the cross in astronomical orientation.

FIGURE 103 • RIGHT
Avenue of the Dead and Pyramid of the Sun at Teotihuacán, Mexico. (c.300 AD and after). The plan of the city at Teotihuacán is based on the geometry of the square and circle.

FIGURE 104 • LEFT
The Jungle City of Toluum by F. Catherwood. The stepped temples of Mexico reflect the form of the sacred mountain.

FIGURE 105 • BELOW
Teotihuacán, Mexico. The temples at Teotihuacán are so much like mountains that hundreds of people can climb them at the same time.

The Pleiades formed a central role in Mayan mythology, and link the Sun Pyramid with the Street of the Dead in the city. During the first and second centuries AD, when the grid plan was created, the Pleiades set just before dawn on the morning of the day when the sun passed the zenith in the sky. On this day, the Pleiades would have disappeared exactly where the sun rose moments later. The midsummer solstice day is the only day when this phenomenon occurs and this influenced both the calendar and customs of the people.

The Hindus created a ritual to establish the cardinal axes, which they identified with the significance of sun and moon.[41]

FIGURE 106 • LEFT
Carving on the Temple of Quetzalcoatl, Teotihuacán, Mexico. The crucified sun god Quetzalcoatl resembles both the serpent and the dragon, two symbols of time and solar energy.

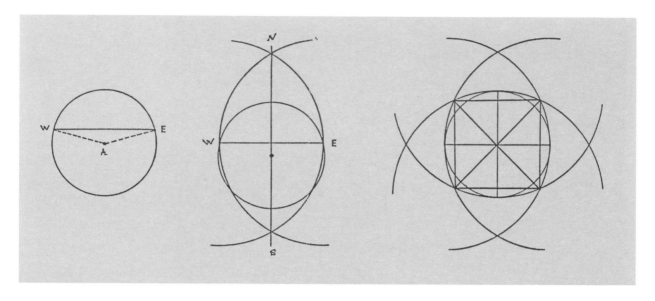

FIGURE 107 • ABOVE
Creating the Axis. A vertical gnomon erected at point A casts shadows AE and AW at sunrise and sunset. A line WE connecting the two points is exactly East-West in orientation. When arcs are drawn from W and E creating a vesica, the orientation of the temple is complete. (After Burchkardt.)

FIGURE 108 • RIGHT
Goddess of Mercy Temple, Penang, Malaysia. This temple not only carries likenesses of the gods and goddesses, but constitutes a mountain of deities.

They first consecrated a position for the altar after consulting the oracles. Next, a vertical post or pillar was erected to act as a *gnomon* - to provide an object from which the sun could cast a shadow. A circle was traced around the post, and during the ceremonial day, often a day dedicated to the god or goddess to whom the temple was offered, the shadow cast across the circle by the extremes of the sun's movement across the sky would determine two critical points. When the points on the circle are connected, they form an east-west axis. When a cord is stretched from one point on the circle to the other, and used as a compass to form two half circles, the intersecting shape is the vesica piscis, a 'fish', which, when its points of intersection are connected, forms a north-south axis. The intersections of the other circles, which are centred on the ends of the cardinal axes, allow the establishment of the four corners of a square.

The circle thus generates a square and the four cardinal points have been established perfectly in relation to the altar.

The square then determines the plan of the temple and its proportions. The god Purusha, who symbolizes the temple, is also the temple itself. He is pictured in the shape of the victim in a Vedic sacrifice: his head is to the east, his feet to the west, and his hands touch the north-east and south-east corners of the square. He is the primordial victim whom the devas sacrificed at the beginning of the world, and who is incarnated in the cosmos. The cardinal axes provided an intermediary place between the circular heaven and the terrestrial square.[42]

Burckhardt describes this ritual of orientation as universal. It is also used in ancient China and Japan, and Vitruvius mentions that the Romans used it to establish the cardinal axes of their cities, after consulting the augurs to determine the geographical location.

Medieval builders used the same process, with some variation, to determine the orientation of the great cathedrals. As the altars lay to the east and the main entrances to the west, the same procedure was used by the master mason

FIGURE 109 • RIGHT
Shore Temple, Mahabalipuram, Tamil Nadu, India. Hindu temple architecture is geometrically profound and makes striking shapes against the sky.

FIGURE 110 • ABOVE
Lakshmi Narayan Temple, Delhi, India. The Hindus use animals and vivid colours in their temples, feeling that in the domain of the gods and goddesses everything is more colourful.

to align the axis according to the sunrise line cast from the gnomon away to the west. This first axis formed the long axis of the building and also meant that on the day of the saint in whose honour the cathedral was erected, the rising sun would parallel the long axis. In this way it is possible to determine the saint honoured in any great cathedral by determining the correct axis.

Often the temple deviates from the true north-south and east-west axes. In Hindu temples, it is considered improper to align the energies of nearby buildings with the temple itself. They see the principal axes and diagonals as sensitive points and vital energy nodes, and it lessens their potency to include them in walls, foundations or pillars. Axial similarity of adjacent buildings is also avoided for the same reason. Transgression causes trouble for the donor of the building and for the congregation worshipping within. As a result, all architectural elements are displaced in a minor way to slightly distort the symmetry of the building. When this principle is applied to the entire building, it is irregular in every element, but the whole carries a level of harmony which is so obvious that it is palpable. The variation from perfect mathematics creates the life of the building and its essential character.

In modern architecture the absolute conformity of shapes, building elements and materials creates an idealized perfection whose artificiality lacks any organic vitality. The ideal shape is too close to perfect for comfort. As Burckhardt puts it:

MODERN BUILDINGS PRESENT AN INVERSION OF THE NORMAL RELATIONSHIP BETWEEN ESSENTIAL FORMS AND CONTINGENT FORMS, THE RESULT OF

FIGURE 111 • ABOVE
The Great Temple, Madurai, Tamil Nadu, India (17th century). Some temples contain a veritable pantheon of gods and goddesses.

WHICH IS A SORT OF VISUAL INACTIVITY INCOMPATIBLE WITH THE SENSITIVITY – ONE WOULD LIKE TO SAY WITH THE 'INITIATING SUBSTANCE' – OF THE CONTEMPLATIVE ARTIST.[43]

In modern buildings too often the subtle currents are entrapped within the structure and its stylized façade, leaving the building itself dead and lifeless. The Hindus see their buildings in a different light – like man and the universe, they have their own unique spirit and soul, which respond to light and darkness, and which act as carriers of the cosmic energies which animate them. The architect confers his/her own spirit into a creation, and participates in the transformation of this ineffable spirit into matter.

The Chinese based their art and science of orienting and siting buildings upon the workings of mysterious earth forces known as *Feng Shui* - literally 'wind' and 'water'. Just as Chinese medicine is based upon interplay and balance between the twelve energy channels or acupuncture meridians which permeate the physical body, so the earth is criss-crossed with energy lines affected by (and affecting) virtually all geographical and topographical phenomena. Meridians carry vital energy, *ch'i*, along specific routes and distribute it by various loci and internal organs connected to external outlets. Hundreds of acupuncture points lie along the meridians.

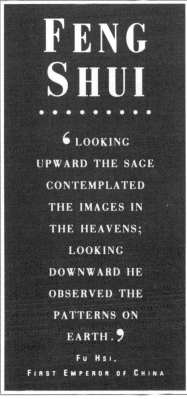

FENG SHUI

• • • • • • • •

❝ LOOKING UPWARD THE SAGE CONTEMPLATED THE IMAGES IN THE HEAVENS; LOOKING DOWNWARD HE OBSERVED THE PATTERNS ON EARTH. ❞

FU HSI,
FIRST EMPEROR OF CHINA

Every earthly and bodily energy channel contains both *yin* (passive) and *yang* (active) energies, and for health and good fortune it is essential to have a balance of the two. The *yin/yang* energies are never separated - everything contains them both in some proportion. The essence of Chinese philosophy as manifest in the *I Ching (The Book of Changes)* is the interplay between these two dancing energies, and architecture is a popular and necessary ground for their interaction. These cosmic currents are collectively called '*ch'i*', the same term which describes life energy in the body. The earth currents are the acupuncture meridians of the Great Mother,[44] who in turn created the polarities.

FIGURE 112 • FAR LEFT
Ming Period Mountain View. The Chinese have always revered the landscape.

FIGURE 113 • BELOW LEFT *On the Li River, near Kweilin, China. The mountainous landscape resembles the domain of dragons and other powerful forces competing with each other for dominance.*

FIGURE 114 • BELOW
Acupuncture Meridians. The acupuncture meridians cover the human body and are lines through which life energy is transmitted. A blockage will result in disease. This diagram shows one meridian stretching from head to toe.

FIGURE 115 • TOP
Mountain Temple at Kweilin, China. This temple utilizes the power of nature to integrate itself completely and naturally into the landscape.

FIGURE 116 • ABOVE
Feng Shui Geomantic Compass. This Feng Shui expert is using the geomantic compass to identify auspicious and inauspicious shapes and objects in the environment for a client.

Feng Shui is a form of geomancy (geographical divination) which utilizes principles such as astrology, psychic and physical phenomena to determine whether the location, form and orientation of a building or monument is auspicious or inauspicious. Buildings which utilize the natural elements of the land and tap into its energy are auspicious places to live, work or bury the dead, while places that are antagonistic to these energies are inauspicious and will not bring good future.

The link with the environment has magical qualities, and the Chinese believe that the placement of a building affects the landscape as well as the other way around. The best possible result is when a man-made object enhances and supports the environment from which it in turn receives energy. Everything in the world interacts energetically, and when sensitivity and knowledge are used together, the blend is universally harmonious and supportive. In this sense it is a shared legacy which anticipates the Green Revolution which is so desperately required today.

• • •

MOUNTAIN DRAGONS

• • •

The mountains which meander across the spectacular landscape of China inspired the early geomancers to liken them to dragons which carried immense power and influence for good or evil over the wealth and happiness of inhabitants of the land. If the dragons in the landscape remained happy then the people living with and around them would prosper, while if the dragons were aroused by

FIGURE 117 • ABOVE
Dragon Mural, Chinese Temple, Malacca, Indonesia. The dragon is the supreme symbol of earth energies.

FIGURE 118 • LEFT
Dragon Dance, Hong Kong Dragon dances are performed to exorcise evil spirits, to bring positive energy to a building or an event and to symbolize a change in fortune for inhabitants of a building.

FIGURE 119 • ABOVE
Mountains and Water along the Li River, Kweilin, China. The landscape of China is often accessible only by waterways between ranges of spectacular mountains. The balance between these two natural landscape elements is central to Feng Shui.

FIGURE 120 • RIGHT
Mountains in Kweilin, China. It is easy to see how such mountains could look like a dragon living in the landscape.

ignorant treatment, they would cause illness and a loss of wealth of the inhabitants, if not destroy them outright.

All natural shapes in the landscape have meaning to the Chinese and correspond to animal qualities which they reflect, so that a particular pinnacle could be a tiger's ear, while a benign mountain might be a protective watchdog. The determination of direction and siting either utilizes these forces or antagonizes them. Not only do they affect the luck of the inhabitants, but it is believed that they determine the prosperity and health of everyone living within their realm of influence. It is everyone's common heritage to respect and be sensitive to the earth energies within which they live.

The two primary natural forms which must be respected and utilized are water and mountains. Water is the essence of life and its processes are critical. The flow, location, depth, purity and strength of bodies of water are all considered and used in evaluating the correct location for a building. Similarly, mountains are considered intersections of earth and heaven,

and as such dispense energy to the surrounding land. In the analogy of the Tao, water carries the yang or active principle, and mountains carry the yin or passive principle: water feeds and nourishes and hills separate and shelter.

In the same way that farming and residential lands must have access to water for many reasons, so mountains and hills are used for special purposes such as siting temples, shrines and burial places. Buildings are sited in relation to the mountains or hills within their view. The axes of such objects are determined and they are perceived as points from which energy either emanates or to which it is attracted. A proper siting taps the *ch'i* of the area at those points where it is closest to the surface, and such places can be easily confirmed by seeing lush foliage, strong trees or rich soil. The veins and meridians of the landscape run down hillsides and across valley slopes, criss-crossing to create energetic nodes of activity.

Certain places tap into the beneficent *ch'i* energy while others are devoid of such benefits and lead their inhabitants to stagnation. Flat valleys, areas without nearby flowing water, or places where the topography is too violent, which could signify a dragon's mouth or lashing tail, are to be avoided. They would bring bad luck and ill health for inhabitants.

The interaction and intrinsic harmony of water and mountains is considered essential to the proper siting of buildings. It is obvious that powerful dragons guarding the land need plenty of clear water to drink! The potency of the landscape can be determined by the flow of the water, and its clarity shows the positive qualities of the *ch'i* it carries through the land, just as blood purity exemplifies the healthy body. However, if the water flows too

FIGURE 121 • RIGHT
FIGURE 121 • RIGHT
Li River Valley, Kweilin, China. The mountain in the centre of this picture would be designated a square, Saturn, earth mountain, while the mountain to its right is an oblong, Venus, metal mountain.

FIGURE 122 • BELOW
I Ching Yarrow Stalk Oracle. The practice of the I Ching involves taking groups of yarrow stalks and determining the six lines which make up a hexagram.

straight or its flow is excessive, it can be dangerous, susceptible to flooding and devastation and therefore an influence to be subdued or avoided.

• • •

PLANETARY GEOMANCY

• • •

The influence of mountains, as well as other geographical and bodily phenomena, can be determined by relating their shapes to planetary and elemental forms.[45] The twelve meridians connect to five energy channels, five organ networks, five seasons and five elements, through which they act. For example, conical mountains belong to Mars and the element fire; round-headed mountains are Jupiter and wood; square mountains are

Saturn and earth; oblong round mountains are Venus and metal; and alive, crooked and moving mountains are Mercury and water.

The mountainous features are combined to interpret the significance and potential of a site in a similar way to that in which the *I Ching* hexagrams are used. Fire controls or dominates metal while water dominates fire. The archetypal qualities of the hexagrams are recreated in the landscape and act in a similar way. Once again, Feng Shui is a reflection of humanity in the landscape and vice versa.

According to Feng Shui the ideal locations are surrounded on three sides by protective hills in an armchair formation facing out towards the south so that the dragon protects the northern sides. The building should be halfway up the hillside and built into it for security reasons.

• • •

THE CHINESE GEOMANTIC COMPASS

• • •

Feng Shui judgments are made with complex and ingenious instruments and diagrams which indicate the quality of directions in relation to natural terrain and cosmic considerations. The Chinese geomantic compass, called the *lo p'an*, is used to orient buildings and monuments in the landscape. It has a compass built into its centre, on the theory that the magnetic effects and the flow of *ch'i* of

FIGURE 123 • BELOW
Lo P'an Chinese Geomantic Compass. This device has a compass in the centre and rings which show the eight trigrams of the I Ching, the 24 azimuthal directional compass points, the 28 hsiu or constellations, the 365 days in the year, and others. The compass is covered with good and bad luck markings.

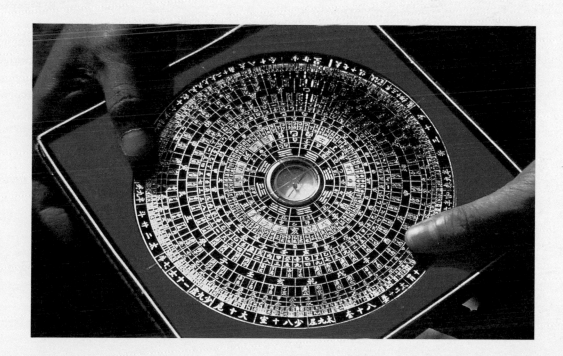

FIGURE 124 • RIGHT

*I Ching Geomancy.
According to the School of
the Compass, the orientation
of the front door of a building
determines its I Ching
trigram. This determines the
qualities of the rooms within
the building. Each room can
thus be described by two
trigrams.*

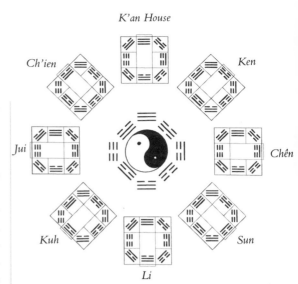

the environment can be measured and described accurately. Because the compass needle is activated by placing it near a lodestone for a period of time, it is believed that not only is it magnetic, but it also responds to the earth energies.

The compass is a circular disc of painted wood, representing heaven, set into a square board, symbolic of earth, and covered with a bewildering variety of concentric circles numbering from eight to forty. Originally the centre was occupied by a symbol representing the constellation of the Great Bear, but subsequently it contained the compass. The rings are based on divisions such as the solar year of 365 days, the zodiacal circle of 360°, the twelve earthly branches, the twenty-eight equatorial divisions or constellations, the eight pricipal trigrams, the five elements in combination, and many others. The various circular dials work together to indicate the correct relationship between natural alignments and mathematical configurations in the natural world, as well as for internal positioning in rooms and houses.

The Chinese system of geomancy which has generated the geomantic compass combines an astronomical-astrological system with its directional logic. In addition to using their own animal signs of the zodiac, the Chinese use the twenty-eight constellation mansions or abodes of the heavens, divided into four sections, with names such as the azure dragon, the sable warrior, the white tiger and the vermilion bird. The various constellations are numbered and attributed to the five planets. Jupiter rules the East, Mars dwells in the South, Venus in the West, Mercury in the North and Saturn in the middle of the earth. These are paralleled by the seven stars which compose the con-

stellation of the Great Bear, which is seen as a large clock in the sky.

The principal agent through which the planets operate consists of the five elements - spiritual essences which carry characteristic energies and qualities. Each element has productive and destructive relationships with other elements, so that a complex interrelationship results. The energy of a person is affected by all these levels of activity, and harmonious life results when all the elements are activated in a balanced way. The male and female natures circulate within the individual, within a marriage relationship and between people and the natural world around them. In peace, all are in concord.

According to the School of the Compass, the hexagrams (of six lines) and the trigrams (of three lines) of the *I Ching (Book of Changes)* correspond to archetypal qualities of life, elements in nature and influences affecting the individual, the family and the nation, and in Feng Shui are used to describe buildings and the rooms within them. Each of the eight possible orientations (to the cardinal compass points and the diagonals) of a building is classified by one of the trigrams, and within each of these orientations, the locations of eight possible rooms are correlated with trigrams. Therefore, any room can be described by one of the sixty-four hexagrams of the *I Ching*, and will evoke its equivalent qualities. One room might be *kuan*, or 'contemplation', while the room next to it could be *po*, or 'splitting apart' - the events in these rooms would subsequently affect the residents in a powerful way.

The energy channels of *ch'i* contained by roads, streams and rivers, and other elements in the landscape and in towns, can be utilized positively or negatively. One way to modify their influence, or to enhance them is with mirrors, which have always had a mystical appeal in Chinese culture.[46] Originally worn in polished copper or bronze on the shield or breast of a feudal warrior, they have the ability to repel negative or evil energies. As such they have a great many uses within Feng Shui to amplify or redirect the *ch'i*. It is thought that the brilliance of mirrors represents and combines the light of the sun and moon, communicating the integrated powers of earth and heaven.

The Chinese understand the universe in which houses and tombs are built as a living, organic whole into which it is the responsibility of every human to integrate. They acknowledge that astrology, geomancy, divination, mythology and magic must combine in order for humanity to live in peace with themselves and with the gods.

More recently Feng Shui has received much attention because in the design of the Hong Kong and Shanghai Bank, designed by Sir Norman Foster, a Chinese geomancer was enlisted to realign major lobby elements in order to create positive energies in the building and benefit the client. The original building design was considered to be detrimental to the environment and also bad for business, probably a more critical concern for the client.

FIGURE 125 • ABOVE
Hong Kong and Shanghai Bank, Hong Kong, by Sir Norman Foster. The Bank was designed by a western architect with the help of a Feng Shui consultant.

While the astronomical alignment of ancient megaliths is of primary importance in linking the people to their gods and goddesses in the cosmos, early humanity located and oriented their sacred monuments and buildings over the landscape according to the forces in the land.

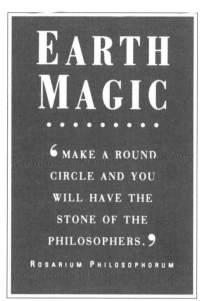

EARTH MAGIC

' MAKE A ROUND CIRCLE AND YOU WILL HAVE THE STONE OF THE PHILOSOPHERS. *'*

ROSARIUM PHILOSOPHORUM

Like the human body, the earth is alive with energies which pulsate across its surface. Just as the Chinese developed their Feng Shui geomancy, a similar prehistoric art for locating and using earth energies arose in Europe. The criss-crossing energy lines discovered in the British Isles and across Europe are called ley lines. Many of the same men who discovered and investigated the megalithic monuments in England also felt that these monuments were, in some mysterious way, connected across the country, and beyond. It was as though there was an invisible pattern inherent in the landscape which determined where such monuments should be placed.

The first group of monuments to be properly studied was the complex comprising the Avebury stone circle, the Kennet long barrow and Silbury Hill. In the eighteenth century these monuments were seen as the work of primitive peoples, but this perception was to gradually change. Dr William Stukeley (1687–1765) was a Freemason and antiquarian who visited many such sites in England and Wales from 1718 onwards and who noticed a similarity between megalithic monuments he had seen and certain Christian places. He also found dragon and serpent shapes everywhere in the landscape. These earth giants lay trapped within the hills, mountains and waters of the land, waiting to be

FIGURE 126 • FAR LEFT
Avebury Stone Circle, Wiltshire, England. The stone circle at Avebury is very beautiful as well as being an example of an astronomically-sited lunar-solar temple.

FIGURE 127 • BELOW
West Kennet Long Barrow, Wiltshire, England (c.2570 BC). The long barrow is part of the complex of monuments comprising Avebury, the West Kennet Avenue of stones and Silbury Hill.

FIGURE 128 • LEFT
William Stukeley (1687–1765), British Antiquarian.

discovered and utilized by enlightened humanity. Stukeley's vision of Avebury as a Druid temple stretching across the landscape is very challenging and also fits existing stone remains.

William Blake (1757-1827), the English mystic and poet, understood the secrets of the landscape giants waiting to be resurrected:

CHAINED WITHIN THE HILLS AND VALLEYS OF HIS NATIVE REALM, ALBION LAY POWERLESS IN FETTERS OF IRON MORTALITY, HIS FORM OBSCURED BY THE ENCROACHING FOG OF A GREY ENCHANTMENT, HIS KINGDOM USURPED BY A HOST OF PETTY TYRANTS.[47]

Blake's poetic vision explored these cosmic spirits, but their traces on the ground were obscure.

• • •

WATKINS AND THE LEY LINES

• • •

Alfred Watkins (1855-1930) was a photographer, inventor and antiquarian who had a great interest in the legends concerning the landscape which were related to him while on his riding journeys around the English county of Hereford. Watkins discovered by a sudden insight at the age of seventy that the many holy places, churches, crossroads, trees, wells, moats, mounds, burial sites, stone circles, standing stones and other sacred monuments across Hereford were linked by a web of lines. These lines were highly organized and stretched as far as the eye could see, usually culminating in hilltops, beacons or mountain-tops.

When Watkins marked out the many ancient and Christian sites across the countryside, he discovered that there were distinct alignments which seemed to follow quite stringent laws. Sometimes these lines stretched for miles, encompassing five or six or more monuments,

linking them together and aligning their formidable energies.

He surmised that this network of lines was originally used as a kind of navigation system at a time when people walked everywhere. The traveller would have seen signs directing the journey which would have indicated the type of line traversed. Watkins found that the place names along leys corresponded to the quality and use of the lines. He originally thought they were lines used by various trades, but eventually rejected this hypothesis.

Watkins unearthed traces of pagan monuments appropriated by the Church, retained in foundations, built upon, integrated into the fabric of later and more acceptable buildings. Places dedicated originally to gods, planets or earth spirits came under the auspices of Christian saints; prehistoric mounds and camps pointed the way between church spires. Formal axes were complemented by natural and overgrown episodes. Watkins understood the entire vocabulary of markers, both man made and natural, by which the ancients marked their paths through the countryside. All these were connected by the names which Watkins traced back into antiquity.

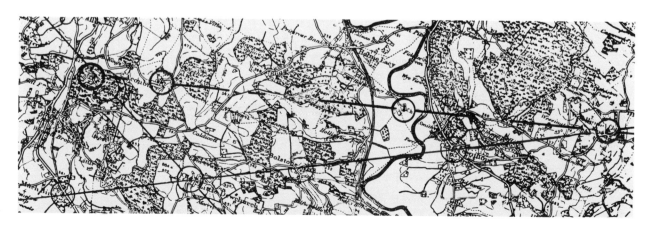

FIGURE 132 • ABOVE
Old Sarum Fort, near Salisbury, Wiltshire, England. The ley line which links Stonehenge and Salisbury Cathedral passes through the hill fort of Old Sarum.

The important ley which linked Stonehenge and Salisbury Cathedral extended over a distance of more than six miles, and passed through the Roman settlement of Old Sarum. Slots in earthworks and a range of natural clues maintain the line and allow the communication to be unambiguous. The magical potency of the ley lines speaks in a way that more recent and obvious alignments never could.

With the restored popularity of dowsing sacred sites in the last thirty years, it has become possible to verify and support the power and correctness of ley lines. Fields of force attend these alignments, dispersing when they intersect, combining and concentrating in stone circles.[48] The energies are attracted to these ancient leys unless they have been broken up by modern ignorance and thoughtlessness. Dowsers such as Guy Underwood have investigated and drawn the energy patterns around and near sacred sites. They all agree upon the power and sophistication of the ancient landscape.[49]

In 1985, I lectured at the British Society of Dowsers annual conference held in Malvern, Worcestershire. One of the other dowsers who had given a talk on map dowsing, Ron Smith from Wales, had heard that an epidemic of multiple sclerosis had been recognized in the Malvern area and that no one understood the cause. He believed the cause to be ley energies which had been improperly dispersed by the destruction of a stone circle. He had therefore map-dowsed the area and discovered the energy lines he considered responsible for the disease.

We were a mixed party of about ten people, from young men to elderly women, and all armed with various types of dowsing apparatus, from hazel branches to coat hangers. We drove around back roads near Malvern until Ron determined that we should stop. He found where the lines crossed a road before passing through a field and up to the top of a nearby hill. There was a clear ley alignment to this hilltop and we could all sense it. When Ron walked along the road across the lines, which were at least twelve feet wide, the force was so strong that it practically knocked him down. When the rest of us tried to dowse it, we all had the same reaction.

Upon following the line to the top of the hill, Ron explained that the reason for the epidemic was that a stone circle had originally existed at the top of this hill, but had been destroyed within the last few hundred years, liberating and dispersing the energy it had been built to channel. The freed energy was so powerful that it had an extremely negative effect upon every living being within a large radius of the circle. When we talked to the farmer who owned the field near where the circle had been, he confirmed that he had always had problems with cattle grazing in this field, and that locals had always considered the field and indeed his entire property as unlucky.

At the top of the hill we saw a wood of young trees, seemingly stunted by some unseen force. We dowsed the locations of the stones and found traces of one or two of them below ground level. The energy we picked up at the circle was chaotic, disorganized and made many of us feel instantly ill. Ron had also discovered that roundabouts often radiated negative energy for the same reasons – they take the linear energy of the roads and send them into each other at uncontrollable angles, producing disarray. The power of ley lines is not just a figment of the imagination.

It is clear that this ley tradition does not end at the English Channel, but extends universally across the earth. Certainly the Feng Shui of China, the Mexican Temples of the Sun, the Peruvian sites, and the Nazca lines all bear testament to the power of earth geodesy.

• • •

DIVINING
AND ARCHITECTURE

• • •

In his fascinating book, *Divining the Primary Sense*, Herbert Weaver presents a concept which has great bearing upon the form, location, orientation and magic of temples and sacred places. He proposed that all objects, including buildings, carry, by virtue of their shape, form or mathematical structure, the quality of either signalling (putting energy out), suppressing locally (within visual boundaries), or suppressing to a wide extent, their energies.[50]

Sanctuary was a requirement of early humanity. Safety involved being protected from the danger of animals or other humans. The chemical or energetic radiations of an individual in a state of fear could be sensed while those of a secure individual could not. In short, Weaver discovered that every creature puts out energies and signals which either disguise or draw attention to its presence. Although it is certainly a sense which has become extraneous to man, early humans discovered ways to avoid detection by animals and others, to cover their tracks and to hide their presence. Weaver claims that the cave paintings of early man were intended to suppress vital signals and to protect the tribe.

FIGURE 133 • ABOVE
African Cave Paintings (detail). The horns depicted here are powerful protecting influences for the tribe.

FIGURE 134 • BELOW
African Cave Paintings. Herbert Weaver believed that early cave paintings were intended to protect the tribe by suppressing signals of their presence.

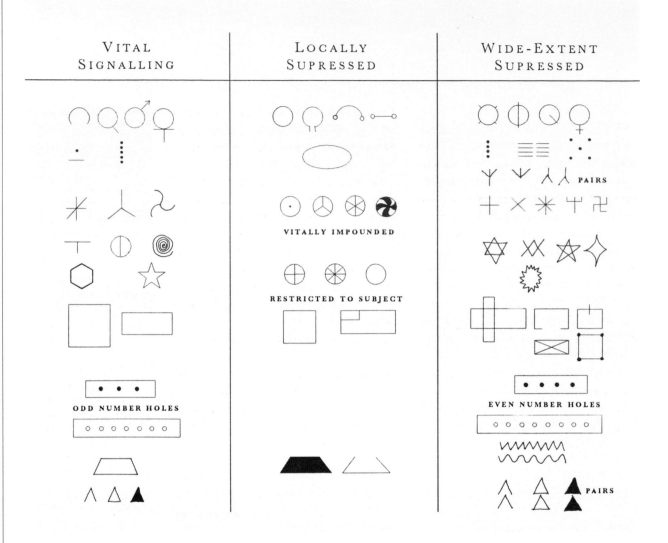

VITAL SIGNALLING	LOCALLY SUPPRESSED	WIDE-EXTENT SUPPRESSED

ODD NUMBER HOLES

VITALLY IMPOUNDED

RESTRICTED TO SUBJECT

EVEN NUMBER HOLES

PAIRS

FIGURE 135 • ABOVE
Signalling and Suppressing Signs (after Weaver). Various signs can be classified according to their force-field character. The vital signs signal and attract benign energies or the favour of the gods; locally suppressed signs suppress potentially harmful sources within visual boundaries; and wide-extent suppressors protect and shield against godlike forces. Signs of serpents and bull's horns are the most powerful wide-extent suppressors.

Certain configurations of objects can either broadcast or suppress specific signals. For example, groups of sticks lying parallel do not suppress, unless there are four or multiples of four sticks in each group; circles only protect within their circumference; while a cross throws a radius of suppression beyond its visible limits. Some such forms are natural, while others were obviously discovered in practice and subsequently used.

Weaver collected and evaluated a wide range of such symbols and found that certain patterns created particular reactions. For example, a law emerged that differentiated between groups with odd numbers of holes, which are vital signalling signs, and groups with even numbers of holes, which suppress over an extended area. When alphabets evolved, the letter signs also carried similar signals. Because of this, certain sacred vowels and names actually possessed energetic qualities which were either life-giving and vital, or deadly and suppressive. Furthermore, religious symbols were not only representations of gods or goddesses, they also afforded protection.

Weaver also found that the shape of buildings and stone circles had specific effects according to their configuration. When joined by straight lines, groups of free-standing stones, such as those at Stonehenge, create Wide-extent suppression, and ostensibly contain the energy of the circle within their boundaries.

• • •

ARCHITECTURAL SANCTUARY

• • •

Safe sanctuary is a fundamental human requirement, the early architecture reflected this need whereas modern building designers do not seem to acknowledge it at all. Crosses, squares, four-multiples and spiral shapes all suppress over wide distances, creating the most favourable conditions for protection and sanctuary. Domes close off a space aurally, visually and magnetically. When walls turn back in on themselves, they provide greater protection than when they just end. Early builders knew that such simple devices could have made a difference as to whether hostile individuals or animals entered the space or not.

Ditches banked with soil, tend to provide underground suppression and even the rainbow symbol provides protection for beings within its arc.

The structure of tents, wigwams and hogans provided the American Indians with protection and suppression when needed. The horns and antlers worn by the warriors also provided protective force fields which prevented chemical emissions from attracting distant foes. Not only were animals and enemies blocked, but it was also possible to protect individuals from the influence of the gods.

The implications of Weaver's ideas are profound and tend to strengthen the significance of certain shapes and patterns used by the early builders of sacred centres and monuments.

FIGURE 136 • ABOVE
*Rainbow at Stonehenge.
The ditches and mounds surrounding Stonehenge and other stone circles provide underground suppression of Vital signals to protect sacred spaces. The rainbow symbol is also believed to provide safety for those within its arc.*

FIGURE 137 • LEFT
Bull Dance, Mandan Indian O-Kee-Pa Ceremony, 1832. In this painting by George Catlin (1794-1872), the use of feather headdresses and bull's horns are powerful suppressing signals to protect the Native Americans from danger in battle and to bring strength to the tribe. The native American teepees look like sacred mountains, or the kivas of the native Americans of the south-west.

ARCHITECTURAL
MANDALAS
• • • • • • • • •

❛ THE SOUL IS A
FIERY EYE ...
FROM THE
ETERNAL CENTRE
OF NATURE. ❜

JACOB BÖHME,
QUESTIONS CONCERNING
THE SOUL

Mandala is the Sanskrit word for circle. Mandala shapes are found in nature in the plant and animal kingdoms, as well as in man-made objects, art and architecture. The earliest mandalas are Palaeolithic sun wheel designs scratched into rocks about 25,000 years ago.[51]

The yogis and priests of early Hinduism and Buddhism, assuming their lotus positions on the earth floor of their hermitage or on the bank of the river Ganges, marked circles around themselves as representations of their sacred space.

The circle within which these holy men meditated was equated to the circular horizon surrounding them, and their location in the centre of the circle was identified with the centre of the world. The sky seemed to be a huge hemi-spherical tent with holes pierced in it, altars were considered to be access routes through which spirits could enter and leave the world, and the Pole Star, around which the whole sky revolved, was seen as the divine tent pole. This cosmic centre coincided with the yogi's own meditation circle or tent pole, the core of his nomadic universe.

FIGURE 138 • FAR LEFT
Buddhist Mandala. The form of Buddhist mandalas is architectonic. The circular lotus floats on a sea and on layers of the elements. The square central section is a platform of the temple, with stupas guarding the four cardinal points, shown in both elevation and plan. Within the centre are successive rings of deities, sacred objects, etc, until at the centre is the deity to whom the entire mandala is dedicated.

FIGURE 139 • LEFT
Celestial Planisphere. The signs of the zodiac surrounding the pole star, from Planis Pharium Sive Mundi Totius Tychonis, from Harmonia Macro Cosmia, *Valk & Schenk, 1708.*

FIGURE 140 • RIGHT
*Measuring a Lunar Transit.
From* Longomontanuus,
Astronomia Danica.

FIGURE 141 • BELOW
RIGHT *Jain Temple,
Ranakpur, India. Such
temples with multiple domes
evoke mountain ranges, with
the primary stupa being an
evocation of Mt Meru, the
sacred mountain.*

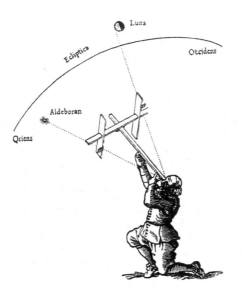

The early personal and individual use
of the mandala gradually assumed higher
and more complex meanings. The most
important shift in content was connected
with the ideal location of the centre of
the universe. Initially, each tent was an
evocation of the centre, but with the
advent of kings and god-priests, the
individual centres became subservient to
more powerful nodes. The stupa temples
and shrines of eastern religions were
centres, secondary to and in imitation of
the legendary Mount Meru, the centre of
all creation. Mount Meru was the intersection between heaven and earth. Later

the Greeks attributed these qualities to Mount Olympus and the Moslems attributed them to the Ka'aba.

The circular mandala form was translated into other uses. As the letter 'O', it was a critical vowel sound in Hebrew and Greek, imitating the rough breathing needed to produce the correct sound. It also resembled the organ of sight, the human eye. This biaxially symmetrical letter was the root of the words *optic, oral, ode, order, opinion* in English, *ops, orion* (boundary) and *organon* (musical instrument) in Greek, and *oeil* in French. In Spanish *orillo* means circumference. This

FIGURE 142 • TOP RIGHT
Vishwanath Temple, Khajuraho, India (11th century). A wonderful example of the Hindu temple as sacred mountain.

FIGURE 143 • ABOVE
Sule Pagoda, Rangoon, Burma. The golden stupa exaggerates the heavenly quality of the sacred place beneath.

FIGURE 144 • RIGHT
Baroli Temples, Kotah. The world mountain stupa is here surrounded by dancing dakinis and surmounted by a globe.

letter also refers to or is a prime component of the words *olfactory, organ, open, ombilikos, origin* and *womb*. Its other combinations include the Russian *okno* (window), and the Latin *sol* (as both the sun and its circular orbit). The Latin *orbis* was anything round, a ring or a representation of power on earth, while *ovum* was an egg. *O* was also the Egyptian hieroglyph for horizon and was used for words meaning 'whole' such as the Latin *omnis,* the Greek *(h)olos,* the Latin *coelum* (heavens) and *orare* (to pray), the English *holy, halo, oracle, omen,* as well as the ultimate words, *Jehovah* and *God*. The circle is at the centre of our being, and the mandala explores the mechanism and effects of this image, as diagrams or in architecture.

The psychologist Carl G. Jung painted and meditated with mandalas throughout his long life, and also encouraged his patients to paint them as a tool for self-discovery. A mandala may be archetypal or may be the externalization of internal issues or problems. Jung

FIGURE 145 • RIGHT
Vishnu surmounting Mount Mandara. Vishnu, the Hindu creator god, sits atop Mount Mandara, the incomparably mighty churn of the Sea of Milk (Milky Way), which is itself on top of a tortoise, symbolizing eternity. The demon asuras on the left pull one way, while the titanic gods and goddesses on the right pull the other way, their interaction creating time through the spinning of the earth's axis.

described mandala shapes discovered in the natural world, such as fossilized sea urchins, moth eggs, and the structure of vitamin C. He also collected mandalas found in primitive cultures throughout history. In particular, he identified tribes or nations which both painted mandala pictures and built buildings or cities upon the same structures.

• • •

COSMIC MANDALAS

• • •

The mandala is a symbolic replica of the world, a geometric projection of it reduced to an essential pattern.[52] In its geometry it acts like a spiritual or psychological wheel of many spokes, each interacting with the centre. By extension it represents the centre of the universe, because the mandala, being the centre, is connected to the Cosmic Centre or World Axis. The axis of the mandala is thus a line of communication between the powers above and humanity below.

The mandala is also an aid to the process of becoming at one with the world and the universe in meditation - the meditator identifies with the centre and allows himself to be transformed by a process of involution.

One of the classic forms of the mandala is the Tibetan Buddhist Mahakala, dedicated to the Great God of Time, (see Figure 146). The outermost circle is a circle of flame, showing transformation and purification, with waves signifying the cosmic ocean out of which the world arose. The world proper rests upon a multi-coloured lotus covered with a series of platforms corresponding to the four elements. The domain (templum or sacred city) of the god is depicted as a square defined by five strips of colour.

From this point onwards to the centre the mandala exhibits the characteristic four-fold and eightfold geometry. Each of the four cardinal compass points is guarded by an entrance gate surmounted by complex superstructures seen in elevation but depicted as part of the plan. Each gate is surmounted by two protective dragons. The entrances themselves contain double-*dorjes* (thunderbolts) which channel cosmic energies to protect the domain.

Within the enclosure are dancing devas protecting the intermediate angles and a ring of the eight bodhisattvas and

FIGURE 146 • ABOVE
Mahakala Gonpo-Magpo Chakra Mandala by A T Mann. Mahakala is the Great God of Time, here seen dancing with his consort on the bodies of his enemies. Surrounding him are the eight sacred objects, the bodhisattvas, the dakinis of the four cardinal directions, all within the sacred temple precinct.

FIGURE 147 • LEFT
The Aztec universe centred around a great god of time.

FIGURE 148 • ABOVE
The Chakras. The chakras are energy vortices along the spine. Each chakra represents a level of being within us, and each is symbolized by a lotus. The number of lotus petals differs - from two petals for the chakra at the base of the spine, to one thousand petals for the crown chakra at the peak of the head. The shapes, colours and forms of each chakra reverberate with their equivalent shapes in nature or in the temple.

FIGURE 149 • RIGHT
Stupa. The stupa seen from above is a mandala, as in this bronze 9th-century Pala stupa from Nalanda, India.

the eight sacred objects. In the very centre of the mandala is Mahakala, the Great God of Time, dancing on the corpses of his enemies and making love with his female consort or shakti, showing his dominance over desires and his mastery of time.

Mandalas such as these are both architectural and meditative. They evoke the natural world, but carry the symbolism of the archetypal world. Buddhist temples contain the same symbolism in their form. Each Buddhist temple is surmounted by a stupa, an abstraction of the solid forms of the five elements. The five elements also have an analogy with the chakras. The Root chakra is a yellow cube representing earth; the Navel chakra is a white sphere representing water; the Heart chakra is a red triangle representing fire; the Throat chakra is a green hemisphere representing the element air; and the Brow chakra is a yellow flame representing the ether. Each of these shapes is also equivalent to a sacred sound.

The shape of the stupa reflects the process of ascent towards unification in three ways: in an archetypal sense; in terms of physical colours and sounds; and architecturally. Thus the architecture naturally resonates with the individual and vice versa. In China the stupas are used to surmount tombstones and burial chambers. The ground plans of many Indian temples are themselves in the form of a yantra, a linear abstract mandala pattern.

• • •

MANDALAIC CITIES

• • •

In a book dedicated to Jung and his work, *Word and Image,* a number of mandala images are shown together with Jung's commentaries. He shows an ancient mandalaic Viking military camp near Trelleborg, Denmark, erected around 1000 AD, which was split into four parts by a crossroads. Within each of these quarters are four enclosures, defined by ship shapes, making smaller squares.

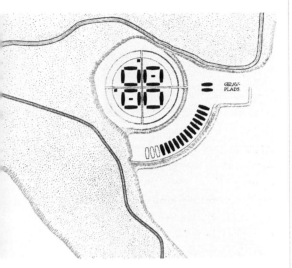

FIGURE 150 • FAR LEFT
*Viking Fort, Trelleborg,
Denmark. The fortified fort
favoured by the Vikings was
a four-fold circular mandala
shape surrounded by a ditch
and mound.*

FIGURE 151 & 152 •
LEFT AND BELOW
*St Sepulchre's Church,
Cambridge, England,
(c.1130). This church is an
eight-fold mandala in plan.*

There are cross-cultural similarities between mandala shapes, as demonstrated by the pre-Columbian city-island of Mexcaltitlan in Mexico, considered by its residents to be the centre of the universe. The ring-shaped settlement is broken up by four sets of crossing lines representing the four corners of the earth. Similarly, a motif often found in Tibetan Buddhist mandalas used for meditation shows identical squares divided into four sections.

Jung had journeyed to the American West and was intrigued to discover Navajo sand paintings which echoed the form of the circular *kivas* or meeting places, also set in the sand (see Chapter 2).

Mandala shapes appear in the earliest megalithic rock tombs, stone circles, burial mounds, primitive buildings and enclosures, forest temples and classical temples.

The geometry and proportion of much church architecture in Christian times is based on circles, even when they are Latin-crosses, as in Western Christendom. The mosque is circular, and the Buddhist stupa is circular. It is only in modern times that the circular mandala shape has been desacralized.

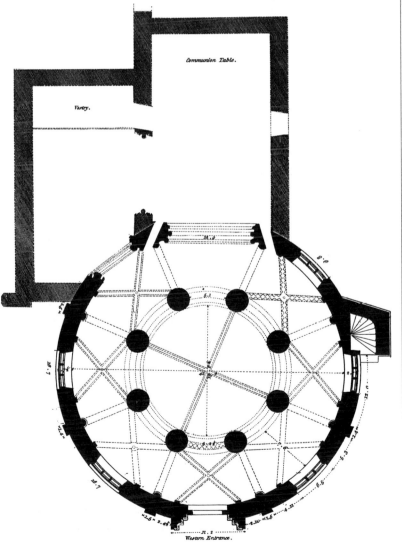

EGYPTIAN SACRED ARCHITECTURE

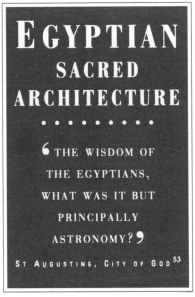

6 THE WISDOM OF THE EGYPTIANS, WHAT WAS IT BUT PRINCIPALLY ASTRONOMY? 9

ST AUGUSTINE, CITY OF GOD [53]

The origin of Egyptian sacred architecture is traditionally linked with the first known architect, Imhotep, counsellor and vizier to the Pharaoh, priest, scholar, astrologer, magician and doctor. He was so skilled in the healing arts that around 2400 BC he was deified as the god of medicine. He was the first to translate vernacular materials into stone-faced ashlar and the pyramid shape and to abstract bundled reeds into columns.[54]

The godlike qualities of Imhotep led to his central role in the mysteries, and his eventual appearance as the Cosmic Architect in the masonic rituals of the cathedral builders. He is also reputed to be the architect of Solomon's Temple, although this is a physical impossibility as Solomon lived approximately 1,400 years later, around 970 BC. The correlation of the architect with god is based on his quasi-mythological character.

Egyptologists, like other scientists, have a vested interest in establishment theories and original thinkers who propose viable alternatives which upset the status quo are regarded as renegades. The primary renegade in Egyptology is the French philosopher and Egyptologist R. A. Schwaller de Lubicz[55] (1887-1961), who dared to suggest that the builders of ancient Egypt had a much more profound and advanced view of the laws of the universe and humanity than anyone in the 20th century had imagined.

The issues raised by Schwaller de Lubicz also make the distinction between mundane and sacred architecture. Instead of interpreting the hieroglyphs as simply letters in an alphabet, and the statues and buildings of Egypt as art, Schwaller de Lubicz understood all three as manifestations of a symbolic language, the original Hermetic philosophy. The sacred science of the Egyptians also expressed the perennial philosophy – it assumed that humanity had descended

FIGURE 153 • LEFT
Sphinx before the Great Pyramid, Gizeh, Egypt (c.2000 BC). The Sphinx and the Great Pyramid are mysteries of the ancient world and could pre-date all other Egyptian monuments.

FIGURE 154 • BELOW
Temple of Philae, Aswan, Egypt (2nd century BC and after). The capitals of these columns in the Temple of Philae are abstractions of lotus blossoms, which symbolize the unfolding creative universe.

FIGURE 155 • ABOVE
Tomb of Nefertiti, Valley of the Queens, Thebes, Egypt (14th century BC). Stars line the ceiling of the Tomb of Nefertiti and rows of coiled snakes show the preoccupation with the symbolism of time in Eygptian religion.

FIGURE 156 • RIGHT
Temple of Karnak, Luxor, Egypt. Detail of Columns. Columns held up the dome of heaven in the temple, and were decorated with symbols of the vegetation which appeared to support the sky goddess.

from a more perfect state and that the object of symbolism is to awaken the original understanding of this paradise state, rather than to educate the ignorant. It is this crucial concept that obviously posed, and still poses, problems for orthodox Egyptologists of a Darwinian bent.

In ancient Egypt the realm of the spiritual was integral to reality, and the illusion of separateness, metaphorically expressed by the Osiris myth, was the fallacy. Schwaller de Lubicz also presented ideas which the mass of humanity are only now beginning to glimpse, and which are primary themes of this book. He (and the Egyptian architects) understood that the human body prefigures all architecture, that the earth acts just like the human body (and vice versa) in having subtle and gross energies crossing its surface and interior, and that blockages produce illness while a free flow of energy leads to health. The temple is truly in man as well as of man. The geomagnetic potentials of architecture and symbolism were explored by those ancient ones, and rediscovered by the grace of Schwaller de Lubicz and his wife, Isha.

The recognition that a temple can be both a reflection of the perfect order of the cosmos and also symbolic of the individual is a theme throughout history, and one which Schwaller de Lubicz finds everywhere in ancient Egypt. Maybe this is why their buildings are so evocative of the spiritual life of our planet for so many people, from so many different and subsequent cultures, and from such a variety of religious orientations. He discovers important and archetypal measures, proportions, correspondences and cosmic integrations at every level and expresses them particularly clearly. In the words of John West:

TO SCHWALLER DE LUBICZ THE TEMPLES OF EGYPT ALSO MANIFEST TERRESTRIAL AND COSMIC MEASURES AS WELL AS A WHOLE GAMUT OF CORRESPONDENCES WITH THE RHYTHMS OF NATURE, THE MOTIONS OF HEAVENLY BODIES, AND SPECIFIC ASTRONOMICAL PERIODS. THE COINCIDENCES OF THESE RELATIONSHIPS BETWEEN STARS, PLANETS, METALS, COLOURS, SOUNDS, AS WELL AS BETWEEN TYPES OF VEGETABLES AND ANIMALS, AND PARTS OF THE HUMAN BODY, ARE REVEALED TO THE INITIATE THROUGH A WHOLE SCIENCE OF NUMBERS.[56]

Schwaller de Lubicz believed that the Egyptians did not develop these concepts themselves, but received them as a legacy from prior Atlantean civilizations. In this way he explains the sudden appearance of

such profound and complete expressions of the unity of things in Egypt, and also the coincidental fact that similar formal cultures in Central and South America created almost identical cosmologies to the Egyptians without any known direct contact. As all such early civilizations,

FIGURE 157 • ABOVE
Great Pyramid, Gizeh. The Great Pyramid seems to have existed in ancient Egypt before the earliest Egyptians and many believe that it was created by the Atlanteans before the collapse of their civilization.

FIGURE 158 • ABOVE
Egyptian Hieroglyphs. The Egyptian hieroglyphs are symbols which express a variety of meanings at different levels, unlike signs, such as the letters of our alphabet, which express only one meaning.

including the Egyptians, believed in cyclical world ages and reincarnation, it is not surprising that Schwaller de Lubicz followed Plato in proposing the origin of the culture in Atlantis. It is significant that the Egyptians worshipped the same celestial, astronomical deities, such as the sun, moon and Sirius, as all the other significant early civilizations.

• • •

THE DIVINE PROPORTION

• • •

The Egyptians used numbers in building, through proportion and ratio, communicated complex spiritual concepts in nonverbal ways. Words can only be experienced in a linear form, whether orally or graphically. You cannot under-

stand a page of words at a glance, but you can instantly get the feel of a building complex. Therefore proportion is capable of a more direct communication.

The creation of sacred buildings echoes the creation of the universe, and both seek to follow similar mathematical laws. Therefore the Golden Section *(phi)* is found to govern the growth of plants and animals, and is also the primary proportion found in sacred buildings and monuments. In their use of numbers as a symbolic language, the Egyptians predate and influence Pythagoras and Plato.

The Egyptians communicated symbolic astrological and astronomical concepts beyond the actual form of the buildings. Similarly, their hieroglyphical language used symbols instead of mere signs. A sign has a limited meaning, while a symbol evokes correspondences and widens understanding. The Egyptians used their mythology to further understanding because it was more than simple history. Their gods came from the stars, bringing wisdom, understanding and power. Their myths were cosmic myths, describing planetary movements, and brought the mathematical reality of the stars to humanity.

· · ·

EGYPTIAN MYSTERIES
· · ·

The myth of Osiris and Isis described earlier describes the yearly cycle of vegetation, as well as showing the relationship between the parts of Egypt, which had to be united in order to overcome the decaying forces of time. In some versions of the story Osiris is contained in a box like the ark of Noah, which itself resides in a great Tamarisk tree, evoking the world tree. But the myth also has an

FIGURE 159 • ABOVE
The Royal Detectives, by Caroline Smith. The arched body of Nut the sky goddess is the night sky, across which the constellations pass. When the sun god rises at dawn, Nut disappears to the underworld.

FIGURE 160 • LEFT
Tomb of Amonchopeshfu, Valley of the Kings, Thebes, Egypt. The animal-headed gods and goddesses came face-to-face with the pharaohs in the tombs of the Valley of the Kings, symbolizing the integration of the lower and higher nature required for divinity.

FIGURE 161 • RIGHT
Dendera, Egypt. The stairway leading to the roof where the priests and pharaoh celebrated the birth of the sun god is bathed in light at sunrise, making the alabaster glisten as gold.

astronomical significance, relating to the Egyptian worship of Sirius. The Egyptians used number, mathematics and proportion to describe every level of this world view, from the mundane to the spiritual.

In Egyptian number symbolism the numbers three, four and five occur often, as they do in their architecture.[57] At school we learn about the Pythagorean right-angled triangle which has sides in the ratio 3:4:5. The Egyptians symbolized three as being heavenly, four as the essence of physicality and earthiness, while five is the number of love and the universe of reconciliation. Schwaller de Lubicz finds the Pythagorean triangle in Egyptian sculpture and architecture, in conjunction with the phi numbers and their resultant Fibonacci series.

Egyptian art and architecture is symbolic. It expresses both artistic and cosmic equations in every work. Symbols chosen from the world of nature, particularly those which clearly reflect the divine proportions, become formal motifs which catch the eye and stun the soul. The accompanying series of column designs show that the lotus, which is the sacred flower of Egypt, and which unfolds in the phi proportion, is often used as the formal pattern in architecture.

• • •

THE MAGICAL TEMPLE AT LUXOR

• • •

Schwaller de Lubicz spent decades of his life at the site of the Temple of Luxor, primarily because he considered it the apex of Egyptian symbolism. It is a magnificent expression of sacred architecture in every way.

The Egyptians assigned body parts to the twelve signs of the zodiac, and the proportions of their architecture reverberated with the human figure. Schwaller de Lubicz related the plan of the Temple of

FIGURE 162 • BELOW
Temple of Isis, Dendera. The mystery of Isis and Osiris is simultaneously a cosmic myth, a vegetation myth and the foundation of Egyptian religion.

FIGURE 163 • LEFT
Temple of Luxor. Columns are abstractions of bunched and tied papyrus or other reeds.

Luxor to a human figure. He believed that astrology was the determining factor in the construction of Egyptian temples.

Schwaller de Lubicz related the organs of the body, the parts of the temple and the phases of history, and considered the whole of Egyptian civilization as a dance through four millennia. He regarded Luxor a perfect example of the symbolic in Egypt, a vast stone monument which expresses the totality of their wisdom - science, mathematics, geodesy, geography, geometry, medicine, astronomy, astrology, magic, myth, art and symbolism.[58] He even found musical correspondences expressed through the proportions of the buildings at Luxor as enhancements to its higher understanding.

The great anomaly of Luxor is the divergence of axes of the sequence of

FIGURE 164 • LEFT
Philae Temple, Colonnade with Capitals. This colonnade shows that the Egyptians used many different capital designs based on vegetation even in the same row of columns, which adds to the richness of the overall design.

Schwaller de Lubicz believed the Egyptian temples to be alive, both in the sense of being based upon natural proportions and also that they oscillate, reverberate and harmonize with humanity, and are, in this sense, a kind of subtle medical treatment device. He felt that the same secret was understood by the builders of the cathedrals, who incorporated similar inconsistencies in their designs. But he knew that these buildings did not just get 'designed', but rather grew from consciously planted seeds. Just as plants create stems according to the Golden Mean, so the proportions governed the increase and

FIGURE 165 • ABOVE
Temple of Luxor, Egypt.
The columns at Luxor reflect
the phi proportion.

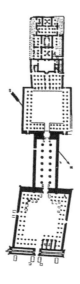

buildings. The shifts in axis at Luxor reflect the changing angle of the Pole Star throughout the hundreds of years of its construction. As each section of the temple was designed and built, the axis shifted, requiring a new alignment so that the rising sun would shine through the wonderful halls of pillars to the shrine within. What is revolutionary about Schwaller de Lubicz's ideas about the axis shift is that he assumes that the Egyptians knew the entire form of the building before it was built, and acknowledged that they would have to adjust it according to the earth's astronomical movements. As they certainly knew about the mechanics and mathematics of the precession, they would have known beforehand and integrated such knowledge into their masterpiece.

multiplication of parts into the whole. This principle also led to the recycling of Egyptian temples, which were taken down when they were obsolete and their building materials used as the 'seeds' for subsequent buildings. He found traces of such 'seedlings' at Luxor. It is as though once its time was served a sacred building was dissolved and its energies redistributed in an appropriate way.[59]

Schwaller de Lubicz discovered a secret which is essential to all sacred architecture: that the seed of perfection lies in the being of man and woman integrated through their love of the world.

• • •

THE SEVEN SACRED CENTRES OF EGYPT

• • •

Peter Dawkins suggests that the Egyptians perceived their land as a 'living temple' built from Nature by the Spirit of God.[60] The structure of the entire country was patterned upon an eternal archetype, fashioned by humanity.

The spine of the earth temple is the Nile, with its head to the north and its body to the south. The seven centres created by the Egyptians are equivalent to the seven chakras or energy centres in the

FIGURE 166 • BOTTOM LEFT *Temple of Luxor, Plan. The axis shifts four times throughout the length of the temple due to its astronomical orientation.*

FIGURE 167 • BELOW *Temple of Luxor, looking from the Avenue of Sphinxes. The axis of the temple shifts many times in its length because it was aligned astronomically and was built over a period of hundreds of years.*

human body, which modulate the endocrine glands, ganglia and plexuses, and groups of organs. Each centre had a specific function and role to play in the education and principles of the whole.

In Figure 169, the chakras correspond to the following regions:

CROWN CHAKRA *Behdet and Heliopolis*

BROW CHAKRA *Heliopolis*

THROAT CHAKRA *Memphis*

HEART CHAKRA *Hermopolis and Akhetaton*

SOLAR PLEXUS CHAKRA *Abydos*

SACRAL CHAKRA *Thebes*

ROOT CHAKRA *The island of Philae and town of Elephantine*

Each major centre had its own cosmology, priesthood and kingship, and expressed its mythology differently. The temples built in each area would have

FIGURE 168 • RIGHT
Rainbow over Philae. Egypt is a 'living temple', the spine of which is the Nile.

FIGURE 169 • BELOW
Egyptian Landscape Temple. The major spiritual centres of Egypt, from Philae / Elephantine in the south to Heliopolis in the north, were correlated by Peter Dawkins to the seven spinal chakras. Each centre had its own unique cosmology, priesthood and mythology and together they created a whole organism.

reflected the geometry, proportions and symbols appropriate to its own set of governing factors, and each was an integral part or aspect of the entire organism that was Egypt.

• • •

THE GREAT PYRAMID

• • •

The Great Pyramid at Gizeh is located at the apex of the Nile delta in Egypt and is one of the oldest monuments on earth. Its functions extend beyond its hypothetical use as a burial chamber for the Pharaoh Cheops (c. 2170 BC). The Great Pyramid has been described as many things: an ancient initiation temple; an astronomical observatory; a telescope; a standard for systems of weights and measures; a surveying instrument useful in lower Egypt; a geodetic marker for the geometric centre of the known world; and the most powerful and perplexing example of sacred geometry of the Ancients.

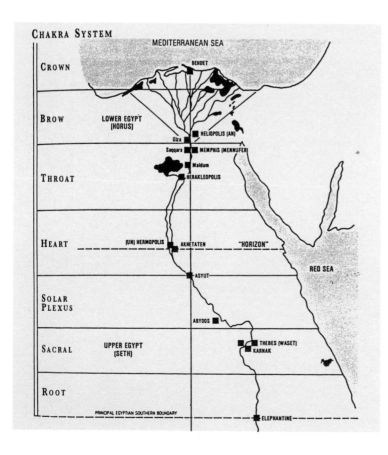

CHAKRA SYSTEM

MEDITERRANEAN SEA

CROWN — BEHDET

BROW — LOWER EGYPT (HORUS) — HELIOPOLIS (AN) — Giza — Saqqara — MEMPHIS (MENNUFER)

THROAT — Maidum — HERAKLEOPOLIS

HEART — (UN) HERMOPOLIS — AKHETATEN — "HORIZON" — ASYUT — RED SEA

SOLAR PLEXUS — ABYDOS

SACRAL — UPPER EGYPT (SETH) — THEBES (WASET) — KARNAK

ROOT — PRINCIPAL EGYPTIAN SOUTHERN BOUNDARY — ELEPHANTINE

FIGURE 170 • LEFT
Alabaster Sphinx. The mysterious sphinx is part lion and part human, symbolizing the solar nature of the divinity, the astrological sign Leo being the sign of mid-summer.

FIGURE 171 • BELOW
Dendera Zodiac. The Dendera zodiac was found on the ceiling of the Temple of Hathor and is the only circular zodiac found in Egypt. Schwaller de Lubicz deduced that it proves that the sign of Cancer corresponds to the chronological birth of Egypt.

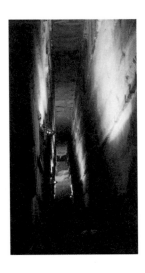

The geometry of the Great Pyramid is justly famous because it has validated the theories of so many astronomers, archaeologists, mystics, psychics, seers and crackpots. It seems as though it is a cosmic mirror, reflecting whatever an individual wishes to find there.

The Great Pyramid remains an enigma because it is clearly different from the other pyramids surrounding it, and from other pyramids in Egypt. It is almost as though it was built by other, earlier peoples and that subsequent pyramids were inferior copies of it, executed by more primitive cultures.

The siting of the Great Pyramid is very special. Gizeh is located at 29°59'48' North latitude, which corresponds exactly to the angle of the Entrance, Ascending and Descending Passages of the pyramid. It required an extremely sophisticated astronomy combined with geographical skills unheard of at the time to site it so precisely. The orientation of the four sides is equally exact. Proctor remarked that the orientation was closer to exactitude than the best observations of the famous Danish astronomer Tycho Brahe 2,000 years later.[61]

The perimeter is exactly one half of the 1,842.9 metres which corresponds to one minute of arc around the earth's equator. The pyramid contained the measurement standards of Egypt.

In plan, section and elevation it is defined by the relationship of the square to the circle - it uniquely demonstrates the 'squaring of the circle', where the circumference of a circle is equal to the perimeter of a square. As the square is symbolically the earth or the body, and the circle the heavens or the spirit, the squaring of the circle is the integration of earth and heaven, and of body and spirit.

The Great Pyramid illustrates the squaring of the circle in both its plan and elevation. When the plan and cross-section of the Great Pyramid are superimposed (see Figure 174) the square ABCD has a perimeter equal to the circumference of the circle with the radius AG, the distance from the ground to the apex of the pyramid. This relationship 'squares the circle' and explains the wondrous power of the pyramid.

The positions of all the interior chambers and passageways are determined by a combination of astronomical phenomena and the squared-circle geometry. When a double square is inscribed within the orthogonal cross-section of the Great Pyramid and projected below ground, the circle which is equal to it in circumference can be created around the centre point M. Thus the square HJKL is equal to the circle radius MN.

The intersection N of the circle and the square is very important because it determines the angle of the Entrance Passage and the Descending Passage, which is parallel to it. Therefore the line MN is parallel to RS. The point where this parallel line intersects the ground line and the double square locates the position of the Entrance Passage. It is one of the primary alignments of the Great Pyramid that this passageway directly sights the major star Alpha Draconis, which was the Pole Star in 2170 BC when the pyramid was reputedly built. This means that when one looks out along the Entrance Passage, this star would have always been in view because the rest of the stars would appear to revolve around the Pole Star. The angle of the Descending Passageway makes the pyramid the greatest meridian observational instrument in the world.

The elevation of the King's Chamber and the Queen's Chamber are determined by subdividing the top half of the inscribed square (a double square) by three. One third up MP is the floor of the Queen's Chamber and two thirds up MP is the floor of the King's Chamber. The King's Chamber is the most potent place within the pyramid   when it was discovered that model pyramids of the same proportions sharpened razor blades, they were placed at the level of the King's Chamber. The depth of the Subterranean Chamber is half the height of the lower half of the square MQ. Point R, where the vertical axis meets the floor of the Subterranean Chamber and the intersection of ground level meet the right hand side of the inscribed square KJ also determines the angle of the Descending Passage pointing to Alpha Draconis.

As a result of the axis wobble, any construction built according to star or planet alignments will gradually become out of alignment at the rate of one degree every seventy-two years. When the Great Pyramid was only 1,000 years old the axis would have shifted by fifteen degrees or more and the position of the Pole Star changed beyond recognition.

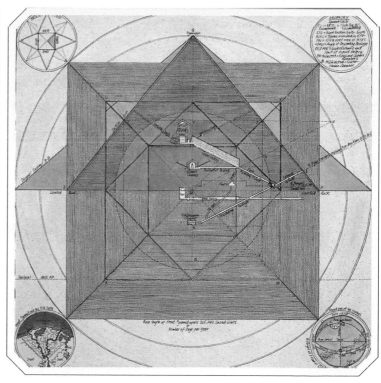

FIGURE 173 • TOP
The Pyramids, Gizeh. Piazzi Smyth hypothesized that the pyramids' site relationship with each other was used as a geodetic device for surveying Egypt.

FIGURE 174 • ABOVE
The Great Pyramid by A T Mann, showing the Great Pyramid in plan, diagonal section and transverse section simultaneously. The passageways are not at the centre of the pyramid, but offset to one side.

FIGURE 175 • ABOVE
The Pyramids at Sunset, Gizeh.

FIGURE 176 • FAR RIGHT *The Great Pyramid as Observatory. Proctor's theory was that the Great Pyramid was constructed as an observatory. If it were built to the height of the King's Chamber, the Grand Gallery would point towards the ecliptic. If a glass lens were moved up and down the gallery, light from the stars would have been focused down to the intersection of the Ascending and Descending Passages, reflected off of a pool inset in the floor there, and up to watching priests at the entryway.*

Piazzi Smyth's famous work of 1880, *Our Inheritance in The Great Pyramid*, contains many wonderfully executed drawings showing the geometry and siting of the Great Pyramid. Among these are two which show the ground plan of the circles of the heavens above the Great Pyramid at the epoch of its foundation in 2170 BC and at midnight on the Autumn Equinox in AD 1881. At the time of the foundation, the Pleiades were on the meridian above the pole, and Alpha Draconis enwrapped the pole, while in Piazzi Smyth's time the polar axis point had moved considerably and the precessional point had moved almost sixty degrees.

Many theories have been proposed about the Great Pyramid and its uses, including some which accept that the units of measurement contain clues to the process of history before and after its

building. Robert Menzies was the first to advance the theory that the passages and chambers in the pyramid, particularly the Grand Gallery, contained specific chronological prophecies, and symbolized the process of Christian spiritual enlightenment. He, and his avid follower Davidson, proposed that the entrance doorway to the Antechamber symbolized the beginning of the final period of Great Wars and Tribulations prophesied in the Bible.[62]

Davidson's book and theories are bewilderingly complicated and intense, and he attempts to prove ideas such as the correlation of events from the Passovers during the Biblical Exodus to the Crucifixion.[63] As an example of this, I include a diagram from Davidson's 1924 book, *The Great Pyramid: Its Divine Message* (see Figure 174). In this great work Davidson shows how events during the First World War and onwards to 1953 are indicated in the geometry and measurements of the King's Chamber *to the nearest day!*

• • •

THE PYRAMID OBSERVATORY
• • •

One of the most astounding and yet strangely logical theories of the Great Pyramid is that posed by Richard Proctor in *The Great Pyramid,* published in 1893. His ideas about the Great Pyramid are extremely clever and perceptive, and are unique in taking into consideration the issue of the axis shift. In fact, his theory has wide applications not only to the Great Pyramid, but also to the Temple at Luxor, and Stonehenge.

Proctor found it strange that the Descending Passage should point towards the northern Pole Star, Alpha Draconis, when the most important observations would have naturally been along the ecliptic, in the exact opposite direction, to the South. Other important questions also remain unanswered. Why does the Grand Gallery have unusually slanted and vaulted walls and deep slots along its length? Why are the passages all slightly off centre to the eastern side of the monument? Why is there an indented cavity in the floor where the Entrance Passage and the Ascending Passage meet? What he proposed provides an interesting solution to all of these perplexing questions. Where other investigators seemed to attempt to overlay their preposterous theories about measurement and time on to the strange architecture, Proctor used ingenuity to discover a reason why.

His solution is simple and elegant. He reasoned that the entire building was used as an observatory, and that the Grand Gallery was the focal point, the chamber through which the observer/astronomer/priests followed planetary and stellar movements. He suggested that the pyramid was initially built only up to the level of the floor of the King's Chamber. If this were the case, the pyramid would look from the top and side as shown in Figure 176. It would be a very large, square platform with the top section of the Grand Gallery penetrating it, slightly off centre.

In ancient times, astrological horoscopes were not made for ordinary individuals but only for kings, queens or pharaohs, as representatives of their subjects. Astrology therefore had a collective rather than a personal orientation. The square platform of the Pyramid Observatory could have been subdivided like the ancient square horoscope. Marker posts could have been erected to act as sight lines for observing sunrises and sunsets, moonrises and moonsets, and the other

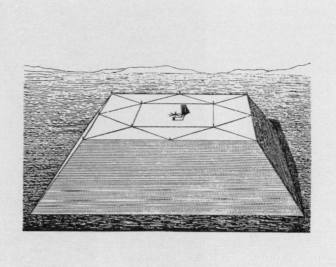

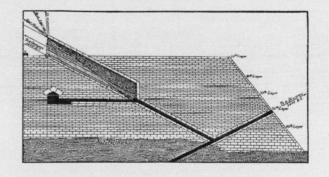

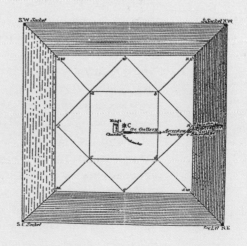

FIGURE 177 • RIGHT
Edfu, Skylit Doorway. The Egyptian architects were masters of light and shadow, and could easily have engineered the Great Pyramid as an observatory.

could have functioned as a mirror for the light rays coming down the entire two-hundred-foot length of the two passage-ways from the stars, reflecting them up the Entrance Passage, where they would have been recorded. The entire operation would have been directed by priests stationed in the centre of the upper platform of the pyramid and at the side entrance. According to the object they were viewing (whether the close Moon or the far-away stars), they could have adjusted the focal length of their telescope, and the dark chambers would have provided ideal conditions for their observations. All in all it is a highly inventive proposal.

In essence, Proctor believed that the Great Pyramid was created primarily as a way of organizing the entire Egyptian nation. The reason for the massive size and weight of the granite blocks, the tightness of their fit and the astronomical qualities and alignments are all, in his view, essential conditions to be fulfilled. The astronomical reasons vied with the sociological, and were the primary rationale.

But, the issue remains, what would have happened after seventy-two years, when the axis shifted and the observatory was a degree or more out of alignment? Proctor deals with this with even greater inventiveness. He proposes two solutions. The most obvious is that the builders simply built over the King's Chamber and continued the construction to the top. His second solution is unique, because he states that *the pyramid was simply taken apart, piece by piece, and reconstructed after adjusting its orientation slightly!* This is how Proctor explains the smoothness of the stones with which the pyramid was made. He claims that the pyramid was built, used, taken apart and relocated tens if not

astronomical events witnessed and measured by these sophisticated priests. The fact that the Grand Gallery was off centre meant that priests could sit and erect a horoscope at the exact centre of the pyramid, adjacent to the chamber.

The Grand Gallery (Figures 172 & 179: The Grand Gallery) and the Ascending Passage would then have functioned as a huge telescope. Being at the edge of a desert, there would have been the perfect materials available to make a glass lens to use in the monument. He suggests that a glass lens could slide up and down the Grand Gallery within a wooden armature, held in place by the slots which can be clearly seen on the sides of the gallery. Since a lens this size would have had a very long focal length, it would have focused the light further down, at the bottom of the Ascending Passage.

Proctor explains the strange slot in the floor at the intersection of the Entrance Passage and the Ascending Passage as a reflecting pool which would have been filled with water with an oily surface. It

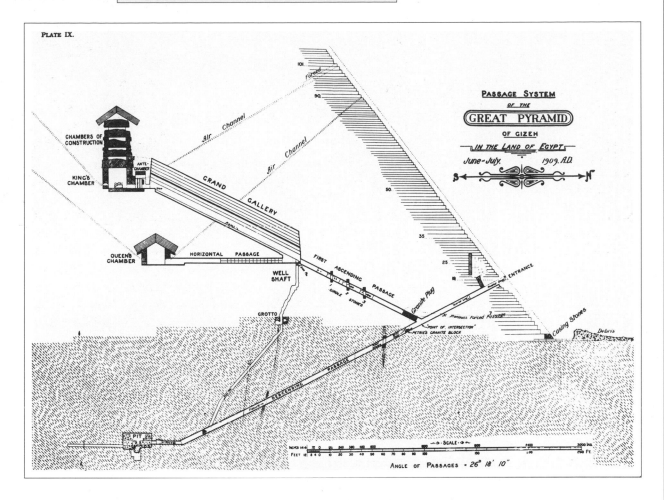

hundreds of times by successive generations of Egyptians. Each time the pieces would have fitted together more tightly, more smoothly, more easily. And, what is more important, the organization of the entire population of the country would have required them to work together to dismantle and re erect the monument. While his ideas are probably quite mad, they are extremely intriguing.

What is most amazing about the Great Pyramid may be read between the lines of the many books claiming its miraculous powers. It is a monument which has such an *archetypal quality* that it manages to verify any reasonable theory constructed about it. Like a dream, it may be interpreted differently by everyone who experiences it, and none of the interpretations are wrong. With this ability, the Great Pyramid must qualify as a major achievement of the tradition of sacred architecture.

FIGURE 178 • ABOVE
Passage System of the Great Pyramid. The angles of the passage system are exactly that of the latitude of Gizeh. As a result, the Descending Passage points to the pole star of the time, Alpha Draconis.

FIGURE 179 • LEFT
Great Pyramid, the Grand Gallery (After LeBrun). The shape and construction of the Grand Gallery is intriguing and supports Proctor's hypothesis.

ISLAMIC ARCHITECTURE

· · · · · · · ·

6 THESE WORDS ARE THE LADDER TO THE FIRMAMENT. WHOEVER ASCENDS IT REACHES THE ROOF - NOT THE ROOF OF THE SPHERE THAT IS BLUE, BUT THE ROOF WHICH TRANSCENDS ALL THE VISIBLE HEAVENS.[64]**9**

SEYYED HUSSEIN NASR

According to the Qur'an, Allah created seven heavens and as many layers of earth, each associated with particular gemstones, colours, qualities, and stages of evolutionary progress. Islamic mysticism portrayed the higher states of existence and creation which lay behind the visible world.

The Islamic tradition utilized such mythic understanding as a basis for its art and architecture. It aimed to transform the universe into an icon which could be contemplated and which would become a mirror of Allah. The entire corpus of Islamic creativity, including the alphabet, astrological signs, numerical symbolism and the science of Divine Names, is a unified structure upon which is based their art and architecture. The mandala diagrams created by the Shi'ite mystical philosopher Ibn Arabi (1165 –1240) utilized geometric patterns for contemplation, and his twelve-fold divisions are a structuring tool in understanding the universe.

Islam also had a tradition of a symbolic and sacred geography which was an attempt to correlate the spiritual world with the mathematical dimensions of the physical world through geographic coordinates. The paramount importance of Mecca, and the requirement of daily worship in its direction, required sophisticated geographic science. In parallel to the Western Tradition, concern with the transition from rectangular to spherical geometries occupied a primary position in the minds of the Islamic builders.

FIGURE 180 • LEFT *Mihrab Ceiling, Cordoba Mosque, Spain (c.961-76). The fantastic integration of dome, circle, square and octagon is characteristic of the genius of Islamic sacred architecture.*

FIGURE 181 • BELOW LEFT *Ilas Bey Mosque, Miletus, Turkey. Islamic sacred architecture is also based on the dome of heaven surmounting the earthly domain, although Islamic architects more often used octagonal or hexagonal shaped sanctuaries.*

FIGURE 182 • BELOW *Blue Mosque, Istanbul, Turkey. Prayers performed in beautiful settings evoking Allah.*

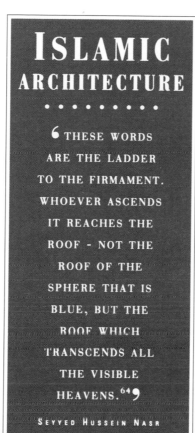

FIGURE 183 • ABOVE
The Ka'aba, Mecca, Saudi Arabia. The most holy shrine of Islam contains a stone which fell from the sky, possibly a meteorite. It is covered by the black cube, and acts as a focus for the eight lines which radiate to the cardinal and intermediate compass points.

FIGURE 184 • BELOW
The Great Mosques at Mecca (below) and Medina (below right).

Islamic mathematics and cosmology occupy a central position in the tradition. Their art and architecture carry the crystalline language seen in mathematical models and diagrams, almost as though it were simply transformed from two dimensions into three. The magic of number contains the message that God is One, and numbers are therefore the most direct route to this revelation. The proportions and sequences of numbers provide the cornerstone for Islamic art and architecture, thus incorporating the mechanisms of the natural world into the artificial world of man-made objects. This essential function of mathematics permeates the entire culture to provide an unparalleled unity and contiguity.

Numbers govern the patterns of tiles, carpets, ornament in mosques and building materials in a unique and positive way. While in the Western Tradition it is necessary to overlay mathematics on to architecture and art, the sacred in Islam is integral to it. The proportions of natural forms are integrated to the extent that the resultant patterns of or on objects have identical structures to natural substances.

The sacred architecture of Islam - in particular the mosque, the Moslem equivalent of the temple - is an image of the cosmos and of the cosmic dimension of the human being. *The human body is the temple.* Body and cosmos are animated by the same energies. In the temple humanity must feel the presence of the Divine Spirit, therefore it must be an image of the cosmos. The house, palace and city are based on similar principles, as extensions of the mosque.

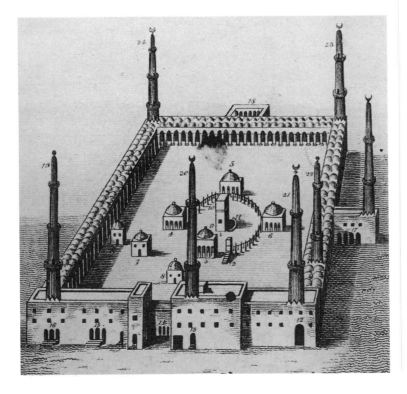

Because Mecca is where heaven and earth meet, all Moslem prayers and sacred places on earth face in its direction, and every precinct in which the daily prayers are practised is a replica in miniature of the Ka'aba itself. The orientation of buildings is as important as their space and form, and their shape and geometry. The square Ka'aba (see Figure 183) is repeated in classical courtyards, which also symbolize its stability and contemplative qualities. As the Divine Throne is supported by eight angels, so the dome of the Islamic mosque is often built on an octagonal base of squinch arches, and can be aligned with the four cardinal points and the four intermediate points.

The symbolic is always integral to the geometry of Islamic sacred architecture, including the use of colours. The colours between the 'beingness' of white and the 'nothingness' of black are symbolic and used accordingly. They are joined by a third colour, sandalwood, a neutral earth tone which is void of colour and symbolizes man and earth. Pure light is unity and the spectrum is symbolic of the diversity and variety of existence. Their four primary colours, red, blue, green and yellow, are related to the elements, the active qualities of nature, the seasons, the quadrants of the day and the divisions of a man's life. Green is superior because it embodies all the others.

All architectural use of colours is a play between the harmonies of opposite and adjacent colours, contrast and complementarity. Each colour expands, contracts

FIGURE 185 • ABOVE LEFT *Shah Mosque, Isfahan, Iran (1612-30). The entire composition of the mosque complex in Isfahan is composed of three courtyards, four porches, seven interior spaces which all interlock to form a continuous spatial whole. The building is a harbour for the soul.*

FIGURE 186 • ABOVE *Caravan of Pilgrims on the Road to Mecca. The need to know the exact direction of Mecca for daily prayers created the necessity to refine astronomy and navigational sciences to a very high degree.*

and moves according to its nature, and the highlights of white and black serve to balance the visual depth and contrast of the colours themselves.

• • •

PATTERNS AND PROPORTIONS OF SPACE

• • •

Islamic architects believe that the synthesis of numbers, lines, shapes and colours provides the awakened soul with a means of expression. Manifestation happens from the centre outward and the spiritual nature of humanity acts from the outside inward. These counter movements appear in Islamic architecture. Walled cities with their four or twelve gateways reflect the cardinal directions or the zodiac signs, and private spaces intermingle with public spaces. Rhythms of openings, avenues, kasbahs and market stalls punctuate multiple axes through cities.

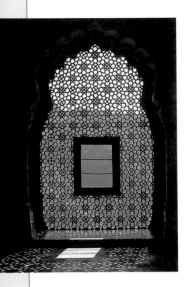

FIGURE 187 • ABOVE
Amber Palace, Jaipur, India. The patterns of tiles and latticework in Islamic architecture show the sophisticated understanding of light and shadow, composition and the creative use of geometry.

FIGURE 188 • ABOVE RIGHT *Jama Masjid Mosque, Delhi, India. The geometry of Islamic architecture is integrated with arches, and views are framed by a multitude of different and intriguing openings.*

FIGURE 189 • RIGHT
Blue Mosque, Istanbul, Turkey (17th century). Diagonals break up the space in the Blue Mosque in Istanbul.

FIGURE 190 • FAR RIGHT *Taj Mahal, Agra, India (1632-48). The Taj Mahal is one of the most beautiful buildings in the world as it changes with the light of every day.*

The four cardinal points, together with the two poles of the vertical axis, provide the six primary orientations and lead to a hexagonal architecture. The geometries in Islamic architecture are symbolic, and the patterns occur everywhere, from the macrocosmic level to the microcosmic level. Triangles, squares and hexagons create their own proportion systems which relate directly with their equivalent elements via the Platonic solids we have already seen. Thus the six square faces of the cube are earthy, the twenty equilateral triangles of the icosahedron are watery, the eight equilateral triangles of the octahedron are airy, the four equilateral triangles of the tetrahedron are fiery and the twelve pentagons of the dodecahedron are symbolic of the universe as a whole.

The primary solid and plane shapes interact using the Golden Mean and circular motifs. Such shapes spiral around each other, playing figure against ground, creating a dance of movement. These proportions are combined in architecture with units of measurement derived from the human body, so that the scale is always right and integrated with the

Patterns of tiles reflect the primary

FIGURE 191 • RIGHT
*Chahar Bagh, Isfahan, Iran.
Detail of Tiles.*

FIGURE 192 • BELOW
RIGHT *Mosque Wall,
Mashed, Iran. Mosaic
Decoration. The mosaic walls
duplicate the geometric motifs
of the architecture.*

FIGURE 193 • FAR
RIGHT *Carpets, Bodrum,
Turkey. Carpets are portable
'centres of the world' and
their patterns represent courtyards, mosque arches, places
of prayer, gardens with
plants and animals, and
sanctuaries. All carpets have
obvious mistakes because
only Allah is perfect.*

inhabitants. Anatomical and astronomical units commingle, and the result is a series of graded proportions in lines, shapes and solids which feel right.

Patterns of tiles reflect the primary shapes of the buildings themselves. Mandala shapes abound and centralized spaces are the norm, reflecting the need for centre, for reflecting the spiritual core of the individual in the midst of an inclement climate. The geometric designs of carpets echo the cities and buildings, and in a way are symbolic of them. The prayer carpets are archways for entrance into the Divine, a place where curves and rigid geometric patterns interact and link, bringing a richness unseen in other forms of architecture and art. Calligraphy is also a primary component of architecture and weaving, making words part of the

FIGURE 194 • ABOVE
*Blue Mosque, Istanbul,
Turkey (17th century).*

vocabulary of patterns surrounding and penetrating the buildings.

The traditional architectural forms reflect the Islamic cosmogony and its sacred texts. The garden courtyard is paradise, the thrones and wall towers reflect the sacred mountain, and gates are entrances to heaven. The axes between minarets show movement through the city and the hemispherical dome evokes the sky. The evocation is complete.

Cities also participate in the same formal geometric patterns. Baghdad was a prototype of the concentric design in the eighth century, just after the time of the Prophet. Square, hexagonal and rectilinear cities contain components which reverberate with the whole shape. Façades of mosques show the entire concert as a play of lively and sacred forms, interwoven into a coherent whole in tune with man and the universe.

FIGURE 195 • LEFT
*Mosque of Ibn Tulun,
Cairo, Egypt (9th and 13th
centuries). The mosque is an
island of sanctuary in the
midst of crowded cities. In
the centre of the courtyard is
the simple dome above a
cube, a perfect meeting of
heaven and earth.*

FIGURE 196 • BELOW
View of Isfahan.

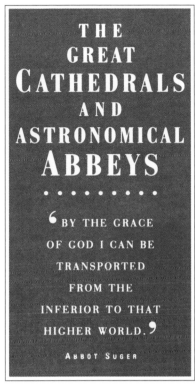

THE GREAT CATHEDRALS AND ASTRONOMICAL ABBEYS

· · · · · · · · ·

❝ BY THE GRACE OF GOD I CAN BE TRANSPORTED FROM THE INFERIOR TO THAT HIGHER WORLD.❞

ABBOT SUGER

The Gothic cathedrals have always inspired awe. We can only imagine the effect they would have had on the local populace in Europe in the centuries when they were built, starting in 1144 AD. The Abbot Suger, entering the first Gothic cathedral of Saint-Denis, built to his own specifications, remarked that the building transformed

. . . I SEE MYSELF DWELLING, IN SOME STRANGE REGION OF THE UNIVERSE WHICH NEITHER EXISTS ENTIRELY IN THE SLIME OF THE EARTH NOR ENTIRELY IN THE PURITY OF HEAVEN.[65]

This statement accurately describes the wonderment felt by all who witness these sacred buildings.

The earlier Romanesque style of architecture was beautiful in its way, but the buildings were massive and overpowering. Suddenly, with the introduction of flying buttresses and stained glass windows, the great cathedrals expressed a crystal-like quality of lightness and aspiration to heaven that was missing in all previous architecture. The development of more innovative building techniques allowed the designers and builder-masons to have huge areas available for light to

FIGURE 197 • LEFT
Notre Dame from the Seine, Paris.

FIGURE 198 • FAR LEFT
East Rose Window, Notre Dame, Paris.

F I G U R E 1 9 9 • BELOW
Abbey Church of St Denis, Paris (begun c.1140). The first gothic cathedral was a daring architectural innovation, combining stained glass windows, flying buttresses, choir vaulting and rib vaults. Inside it glows with coloured light, like a jewel of heaven on earth.

flow into their central spaces, bringing a new quality and magic to Christianity.

While the majority of these great buildings are in France, they were also built in England, Germany, Italy and Spain over a period of less than two hundred years. The reason they suddenly appeared is based in the rise of the language of symbolism. Painton Cowen identifies the great leap in imagination from a building occupying space to a Church signifying power in *time*. The cathedrals were oriented around the Incarnation and Crucifixion of Jesus Christ at the altar in the New Testament, with the north side representing the Old Testament and the south side representing the Last Judgment and the New Jerusalem. They formed a Latin cross, the ship or ark of Noah which saved all life on earth during the Great Flood. The nave reflects the sacred vessel which carries humanity through time, and the rose windows guide that course. The symbolism of the cathedral with rose windows carries profound meaning at many levels.

• • •

THE CHARTRES SCHOOL

• • •

The Chartres School was more than an architectural movement – it was an integration of the ancient mystery schools with influences from Pythagoras, Plato, Plotinus, Augustine, biblical prophecy, the emerging archetypes, and pagan elements from the unconscious, all within a new architectural vocabulary. As an intellectual movement it had no equal, and was the vehicle by which the eastern influences of Arabic and Semitic philosophy came to the West. It is not accidental that the rise of the Chartres School coincided with the Crusades.

FIGURE 200 • LEFT
Chartres Cathedral, South Façade (c.1227). This rose window depicts Christ as described by St John in the Book of Revelation, the 24 elders of the apocalypse, and a crown symbolizing the martyrs who died for Christ.

FIGURE 201 • ABOVE
Abbot Suger of St Denis, Paris (c.1081-1151). The abbey church of St Denis, the first gothic cathedral, was built in Paris to his specifications.

The primary principle behind the movement was that number provided a meaning through which the Divine could be communicated to the mundane world. The axiom of the Chartres school was that just as all numbers derive from One, so all things emanate from God.[66] The message of creative evolution derived from the Bible, both the Old and New Testaments, was the keynote of the cathedrals and the schools, an incarnation of number and geometry in humanity. The School was ordained to transmit a new level of understanding about the way in which the world was created, and provided a vehicle for higher understanding as expressed through its sublime architecture.

The cathedrals, together with their rose windows, are beautifully clear expressions in stone, glass, light and colour, all integrated with perfect proportions and dimensions, of spirituality on earth. They were also profound teaching devices designed to make clear to the mainly ignorant lay people the stories and mysteries of Christianity in a way that they could not fail to understand. The essence of this transmission is the expression of the *Logos*, the 'word of God', represented by Christ.

FIGURE 202 • ABOVE
Chartres North Rose (c.1233). This window is generated from the square and the circle, and therefore is one of the purest roses geometrically. The 12 squares rotate and read with each other to form three major squares which organize the entire window.

• • •

THE ROSE WINDOWS

• • •

At Chartres Cathedral number and proportion were used in a way which transcended the building itself. It is as though a new language emerged which was able to express a higher aspect of the human spirit. The prime representation of this was in the geometric relationship between the rose windows and the maze inscribed on the floor of the nave. The geometry of the rose windows brings ancient principles together with Christian ideas in a complete, compelling and illuminating whole

The rose itself is a powerful symbol which evokes soul, eternity, wheel, sun, cosmos, universe, alchemy and love. It is the supreme western symbol of enlightenment and the redemption of humanity, similar to the lotus in the eastern religions, and in both cases the unfolding of the flower is a symbol of the development and attainment of higher spiritual understanding. The rose was sacred to Isis, Aphrodite and Venus as a symbol of human love transcending passion, and signified the Virgin Mary in Christianity, as well as being the central image of the Rosicrucians. The rosary is also derived from the rose symbol.

The composition of the rose windows in Chartres is extremely important. The three major windows in the cathedral are the North Rose, with the Virgin and Child in the centre, the South Rose, dedicated to the New Testament and the martyrs who spread the Word, and the West Rose, which features the wounded Christ at the centre of the Last Judgment. Each window uses the same vocabulary of colour, form, geometry and symbol, but with a flavour which uniquely expresses its own spiritual intention.

The different quality of light coming from each direction affected the colour of glass used in the windows. North light is quite cold, and therefore in the North Rose the colours red and blue predominate with gold and white support. By contrast in the South Rose, where the colour of the light is warmer due to its exposure, the gold and white are more in evidence and provide a lighter and more dramatic effect.

FIGURE 203 • ABOVE
St Chappelle, Paris (1243-8; rose window 15th century). The rose window at St Chappelle is most like a multi-faceted gem of many colours, glistening in the sunlight and symbolizing the many faces of God on earth.

FIGURE 204 • FAR LEFT
Church of St Francis of Assisi, Italy (c.1250). This Italian window faces the rising sun and demonstrates the motif of wheels within wheels.

FIGURE 205 • LEFT
Reims Cathedral, France (begun 1210). The interior vaults recall the bunched papyrus columns of the Egyptian temples.

• • •

CRYSTAL ALCHEMY

• • •

The glass itself is of immense importance in the rose windows. While most assume the colour is critical, it was believed that the windows were capable of having a much more profound effect. Since this was the time of the rise of alchemy, it was believed that the light passing through the windows was transformed or transmuted and therefore had a healing and revivifying effect upon the people gathered within the cathedral.

Glass before this time was usually painted, and lacked sufficient depth or power to create powerful effects. The glass at Chartres was believed to have been made by the alchemists. Part of the reason for this was that each colour was created by introducing metallic powders to the glass, and gold was used to produce certain red shades. Glass-making was a heavily guarded secret known only to the few members of its medieval craft. The science and aesthetics of the process inter-mingled until it was impossible to tell which craftsman was responsible for the overall effect. What is certain is that the glassmakers' art in stained glass windows reached its acme at Chartres, but only lasted for a brief time before it was debased after the thirteenth century.

Ingredients were added at special stages of the glassmaking process; it was melted to specific temperatures, blown to thin it, and combined with other materials to strengthen and purify it. The metallic oxides were added to produce the colours: Bohemian cobalt oxide for blue, copper oxide for red, and silver chloride for yellow.[67] The impurities and vagaries that resulted from making the glass by hand were of great benefit because it was these qualities that gave the windows their character. The craftsmen used everything they could about the material to create the most powerful and impressive visual pyrotechnics.

Once the glass was coloured and cut to size, it was placed within the leading and often further painted, treated, shaped, fitted or layered to create the desired effect. Apparently some of the pieces of original glass in Chartres had over forty layers of flashing, giving subtle variations of tone in the window. The Abbot Suger boasted that the 'most precious variety' of glass was made by placing sapphires in the melt to colour the glass at St Denis.

The colour schemes were also very important. Although due to limitations of the technology red and blue were the predominant colours, there was an entire spectrum to work with and it was used with great care and attention to the overall balance and effect. The gem-like transmutation of the light through these windows created a truly transcendental effect which can still be felt today.

• • •
ROSE WINDOW DESIGN
• • •

The design of the rose windows was carried out by a team of craftsmen led by the master mason, the co-ordinator of the entire building. For the windows the subject matter would have been chosen by the clergy working with the master, and then carried out by the blacksmith and glazier. The vocabulary of forms was quite standard, and even the posture and disposition of the figures and backgrounds were traditional. There was, nonetheless, very wide scope for creativity, particularly in the geometry which formed the framework of the design.

The most common motif of the rose windows is naturally the circle and the cross. This created a radiating pattern which was effected by either the stonework surround, the leading of the glass, or a combination of the two. The predecessors of the cathedral roses were simple circular holes in the walls *(oculi)* which were used in many Romanesque buildings right down to village churches, and examples of these occur throughout Provence and Tuscany. Some of them are decorated with carved stone figures, such as the wonderful window at Tarascon (see Figure 207), which includes the figures of the four evangelists: the Lion of St Mark, the Bull of St Matthew, the Eagle of St

FIGURE 207 • LEFT
Oculus Rose, Saint Gabriel, Tarascon (c.1180). Tarascon shows the predecessor of the rose window, the oculus richly carved around its perimeter. It is surrounded by the symbols of the four evangelists.

Luke and the Angel of St John. The composition of this window is the circle within the square, symbolizing the role of the evangelists in furthering the integration of heaven and earth.

The wheel was used in Romanesque churches, glazed with thin sheets of alabaster or primitive forms of glass. Early windows were sectioned in quarters, then other segments were made by division, until the whole represented a wheel with a hub and radiating spokes. A curious window mentioned by Cowen is in the form of the Wheel of Fortune at Saint-Etienne, Beauvais.[68] The tarot card of the Wheel of Fortune (see Figure 211) is an image which was often used in medieval times to illustrate the randomness of life and the action of what is called the 'wheel of karma' in the East. The repetition of day and night, the four seasons and the cycle of death following life were primary factors in the rise of Christianity. This religion provided a release from this eternal wheel of suffering, and inspired the spiritual integration which would bring peace and transcendence.

The early roses were primarily stone with glass inset, but later windows after 1180 AD seemed to be clear expanses of circular glass and created an even more magical effect. When the second giant West Rose at Chartres was completed, its diameter of forty-six feet was crosshatched by limestone tracery which was like a filigree and seemed magically suspended in space - exactly what the builders had in mind.

FIGURE 208 • BELOW
Beauvais Cathedral, France (begun 1225). The south rose window at Beauvais represents the Creation according to Genesis in its innermost petals and subsequent Biblical stories until the Exodus. As Painton Cowen states, it symbolizes our intimate connection with nature.

LA ROUE DE FORTUNE
THE WHEEL OF FORTUNE

• • •

GEOMETRIC ROSES

• • •

It is in the geometry of the rose windows that the true magic is made manifest. Each window has its own unique geometrical composition underlying its form. While the viewer does not immediately see the organizing principles and geometric dynamics, with examination it is possible to find the rationale for all the shapes, their positions and interrelationships.

In 1979, at the request of my friend Painton Cowen, we undertook an analysis of a number of the rose windows for his book. The results of these studies show that the richness and subtlety of the geometry is indeed inherent in the form and structure of the windows. It is not known how they were designed, but since I had heard that they were not constructed from measured drawings until after the geometry had been worked out, I decided to adopt this technique myself. It was an illuminating experience.

FIGURE 209 • ABOVE
Wheel of Fortune, Beauvais, Saint Etienne, (c.1100). The carved stone tracery around the window depicts the Wheel of Fortune, a common element of tarot cards which were to be produced two centuries later. This image shows a spinning wheel of life and rebirth, with various creatures ascending one side and others falling down the other. It is a profound symbol of life and spirituality.

FIGURE 210 • TOP LEFT
Wheel of Fortune. A card from the Mandala Astrological Tarot by A T Mann, shows the image as a mandala.

FIGURE 211 • LEFT
Wheel of Fortune. The traditional representation of the Wheel of Fortune.

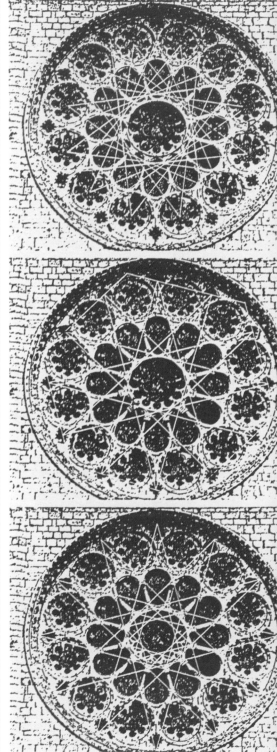

FIGURE 212 • ABOVE
Chartres Cathedral, West Front. The West Rose at Chartres, built in 1216, is over 14m in diameter and is a standard by which other roses have been judged. It has limestone tracery designed in a precisely geometric form enclosing 12 rosettes with blue and red glass.

FIGURE 213A, B & C
RIGHT *Chartres Cathedral, West Rose Geometry. The geometry of the windows is very precise. Five separate systems of proportion rhythmically organize the wheel.*

• • •

CHARTRES WEST ROSE

• • •

The West Rose at Chartres is a classic window because of its rhythmic structure as well as the glass within it. The proportional systems used to construct it interact in a way which could be considered perfect. It is therefore worthwhile to see how the geometry functions.

The basic geometry of the window is twelve-fold. There are twelve of each element, although they are of different sizes and relationships to each other. The most basic proportion is in the radius from the centre of the window to the centre of the particular window element. In Figures 213A, B and C, the geometrical pattern is shown as a white overlay upon a photograph of the window.

The large outermost rosettes (A) are created in a natural and logical way by dividing the circle into twenty-four parts and then making a twenty-four-sided star. This is constructed by drawing a line from the starting point to a position nine positions along in a clockwise direction. By continuing this action, a continuous figure is generated. The points alternate between the centres of a rosette or the tracery (B) between them. In the centre of the window, a series of rotating squares twelve feet per side defines the central circle (C). This star shape also determines the position of the next layer of twelve archways (D). The star tines are tangent to these shapes.

The inner cornice (E) is defined by connecting the centres of the small lights (F) at the outermost edge of the window. This star is also tangent to the twelve archways (D) and to the rosettes (A). A hexagon inscribed around the star defines the perimeter carved leaves, with an individual leaf denoting the exact spot. The star also creates a series of squares (or hexagons) in the centre of the window defining the central circle (C).

Another twelve-pointed star can be constructed from the apex of the little perimeter lights, which again defines the central circle. All the intersections fall on the columns, and the outermost define the positions of their capitals. When equilateral triangles are constructed from the apexes of the innermost dodecahedron, the innermost glass circle is finally identified, and the geometry is complete. This analysis was carried out by John James to a margin of error of ±2 cm.[69]

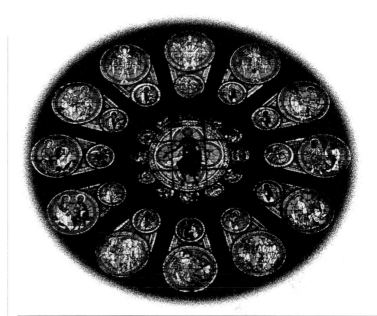

FIGURE 214 • TOP
Chartres Cathedral, West Rose, Detail. Christ is at the centre surrounded by 12 lights containing four symbols of the Evangelists and eight angels and seraphim. Next are the 12 apostles arranged in pairs and the dead rising from tombs.

FIGURE 215 • ABOVE
Chartres Cathedral, West Front.

FIGURE 216 • BELOW
Chartres Cathedral, North Rose Detail. The Virgin holding the Christ child is at the centre of this magnificent rose window.

• • •

CHARTRES NORTH ROSE

• • •

The most representative window of the earliest and most powerful geometric alchemy is the North Rose at Chartres. In a painting I later made of this window, I constructed the entire window geometry using only a straight edge and a compass. The Chartres Rose illustrates many important principles relating to rose windows, but its geometry is the finest - everything is generated by the interaction of the square within the circle.

The North Rose is unusual and profound because of the myriad squares used to create the geometry which simultaneously radiates and spirals from the centre outward and vice versa. All the squares are aligned with radii of the circle, shifting in size as they step toward the centre of the rose. The initial points from which the entire geometry evolved is the series of twelve small circular lights around the periphery of the window. The position of these lights is determined by the masonry outside. The centres of the circles of the circular lights are used to position the expanding and diminishing squares. If a straight line is drawn connecting the centre of each of the adjacent circular lights at the periphery, a square may then be created and positioned from the resultant diagonal. The innermost points of the outermost squares may then be joined to determine another set of diagonals which are again used to create squares of a smaller size. By continuing the process all the way into the centre of the rose window, the entire geometry becomes clear.

The series of squares is an expression of the ultimate organizing geometry, the Golden Mean. When drawn into the centre, the intersecting points of the sets of squares produce a spiral which is governed by the Fibonacci series (where each term is the sum of the two preceding terms). Not only does the spiral reflect the Golden Mean, but the sizes of the squares as they step into the centre also diminish by the same proportion.

The spiralling, stepping, rotating progression of squares into the centre of the rose can be connected to create a golden spiral as in Figure 217. The window is thus not only called a rose window, but its geometry simulates the growth pattern of unfolding of the rose flower. There are twelve groups of spirals which follow this mathematical law, although only four of them are shown in the accompanying figure (see Figure 217).

THE OUTER LIGHTS ARE BOUND WITH THE TWELVE KINGS, ANGELS AND DOVES TO GIVE BIRTH TO THE LOGOS AT THE CENTRE. THE CREATIVE LOGOS OF THE UNIVERSE, THE LAW OF NATURE, IS FOLLOWED BY MAN TO GIVE PERFECT BEAUTY.[70]

Other mathematical organizations occur within the windows besides the sunflower pattern. In Figure 218A the size and location of the semicircular outermost lights are determined by truncated interlocking equilateral triangles. The intersecting triangles also define interlocking squares which spiral around the centre and link the square openings with the quatrefoils. Since the triangles originate off the circle of the window, they help to bind it with the building mass.

When a system of straight lines is drawn connecting every fourth inner circular light, another series of interlocking squares is created which defines the semicircular outermost lights. In addition, a series of squares joining the centres of every fourth quatrefoil defines the centres of the squares. (see Figure 218B).

When the squares of this window are observed, particularly in their natural colours and with pure light penetrating them, the square organization seems to move and shift in an angular way so that the entire window comes alive. Meditation on this window can create a state of mind within which the symbolism of the window shines through. The unconscious forces at work create a layer of intense energies through the interlocking squares which require a level of concentration and focus of which very few people are capable. The magic which results from these relationships cannot be explained in any rational way, but is a powerful ingredient in the building's alchemy.

The geometry of interlocking squares and triangles evokes astrological principles, and because the window is based on a twelve-fold geometry, it is natural to correlate it with such cosmic symbolism and meaning. Thus the Virgin (Virgo) and Christ (Pisces) signify the opposition which characterized the Piscean Age which we are now closing as the Aquarian Age begins. The geometry of this window not only expresses a pleasing aesthetic, but also identifies the precessional age of Christianity itself.

FIGURE 217 • ABOVE
Chartres Cathedral, North Rose Geometry by A T Mann. The spiralling squares increase from the centre out, according to the Golden Mean and generate a spiral also expanding in a Golden Mean proportion.

FIGURE 218A & B •
LEFT & RIGHT
Chartres Cathedral, North Rose Geometry. The patterns of interlocking squares which extend beyond the circle of the window in (A) (left) serve to bind the window to the surrounding building in an intimate way, while the smaller interlocking squares in (B) (right) rotate and shift, creating visual intensity and movement.

FIGURE 219 • RIGHT
*Chartres Cathedral, South
Front*

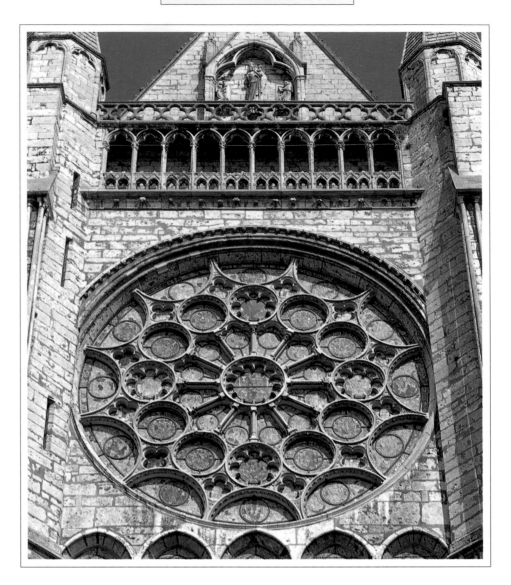

• • •

CHARTRES SOUTH ROSE

• • •

The South Rose at Chartres (see Figures
220 & 221) also has a twelve-fold geometry. The geometric pattern is perceived
by a casual observer if not actually identified in its full complexity of form. When
squares are inscribed within the outer
circle of the window between the semicircles, their intersections define the positions of quatrefoils and are tangent to one
of the major inner ring of circles. When
the centre of every fifth semicircle is connected by a continuous line, the resultant
intersections define the minor inner ring
of circles – each line is tangent to four of
these circles, as well as being tangent to

the outer ring of circles. When the centre
of a semicircle is joined with the extreme
edges of the semicircle opposite, the
resultant lines define the central circle
containing the figure of Christ and the
outer edges of the outer circles. Each one
also traverses a quatrefoil, and the intersection of two defines their centres.
There are undoubtedly even more geometric systems at work within these mas-
terpieces of sacred architecture.

The interplay of such geometric games
makes for a lively visual sensation, and
serves to integrate the symbolic images
reposing in each of the single elements of
the overall composition. The linkage of
images, colours and subject matter
through a geometry like this is profound.

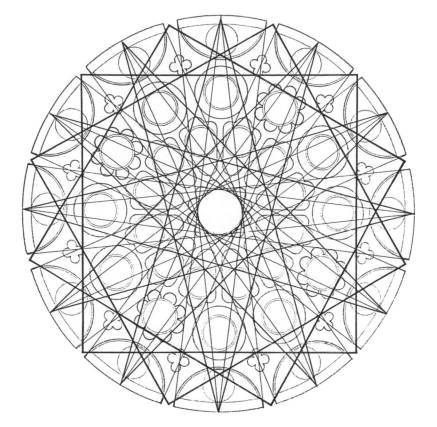

FIGURE 220 • LEFT
Chartres Cathedral, South Rose Geometry. The geometric patterns which exist within the rose window are often subtle and act subliminally to entrance the beholder. Here the semicircles around the edge unconsciously 'focus' the eye on the centre. The pattern of lines defines the positions of the central medallion enclosing Christ and the small quatrefoils, and is tangent to others. Again, there are many interpenetrating squares surrounding the centre - the motif of square and circle is omnipresent.

FIGURE 221 • LEFT
Chartres Cathedral, South Rose (c.1227). The changing colour spectrum and rotating geometry gives this window great vitality and spirituality simultaneously.

• • •
NOTRE-DAME PARIS NORTH ROSE - THE ALCHEMIST'S ROSE
• • •

The North Rose at Notre-Dame in Paris is called the 'Alchemist's Rose', we can surmise because of the supreme quality and invention of its geometry. Each concentric layer of circles and other shapes are built up of geometric intersections which originate with the previous layer, making for an integrated whole which creates a powerful visual phenomenon.

The outermost ring of thirty-two circular trefoil lights appears to be almost random because they alternate in and out. By joining the centre of every eighth window and continuing the process, an endless shape is created which integrates all these lights with the next ring of circular shapes. Each of these next medallions is defined not only by its centre, but also by two tangent lines. The next layer is defined by a similar process but using every eleventh medallion, creating two interlocking sixteen-pointed stars; and these define the centres of the sixteen central windows representing the Christian prophets.

When lines are constructed from the centres of the prophets' circles, four interlocking squares may be seen, producing by their tangents the red and gold halo around the Virgin and Child in the centre. The limits of the central rosettes are also defined by the extent of these lines. The overall impression of integration that this window conveys, as if by magic, can be seen in this light to be a creation of the geometry of the rose window in its most profound form.

The geometry relates every part of the window to every other part in turn, and the numerology of the relationships can be designed and interpreted by those that know, and everything is focused upon the centre, the unifying core of the symbol, the female and male, Virgin and Child.

• • •
ZODIACAL WINDOWS
• • •

Many of the rose windows, including the Chartres North Rose, contain astrological symbolism. Christ is often shown at the centre of the circle of zodiac signs, representing his medieval position as a synthesis of the astrological round. The zodiac is a significant representation of the powers of the unconscious, and the Christian consciousness embodies such qualities in a higher union. Jung identified St John's 'seven stars' as the seven planets and as symbols of the unconscious.

FIGURE 222 • FAR LEFT *Notre-Dame, Paris, North Rose (c.1268). Called the 'Alchemist's Rose', this is a supreme example of the workings of the invisible geometry acting within the rose windows.*

Figure 223 • TOP LEFT *Lausanne Cathedral, Switzerland. This detail shows the astrological sign Scorpio.*

FIGURE 224 • BELOW *Notre-Dame, Paris, North Rose Geometry. Dynamic, tangental geometry connects each concentric ring of elements to the next. The outer geometry links every eighth light, thus creating the tangents that define the positions of the 32 inner medallions. Next, by linking every eleventh medallion, two interlocking sixteen-pointed stars are created. The process culminates in a halo of colour with the Virgin and Child at its centre.*

FIGURE 225 • ABOVE
Gold Statues, Venice.
Churches carry profound
astrological and cosmological
symbolism. Here the golden
St. Mark surmounts an
abstract world mountain,
flanked by golden angels, all
showing the higher spiritual
reality of Christianity. Below
Him a golden winged lion
flies against a backdrop of
stars, showing the symbolism
of St. Mark as a solar deity,
linking His astrological and
spiritual origins.

FIGURE 226 • BOTTOM
RIGHT *'Christ in Majesty'*
(c.1220). This design from
a psalter and prayer book car-
ries the astrological symbols of
the four Evangelists, showing
the intimate integration
between Christianity and
astrology.

FIGURE 227 • BOTTOM
FAR RIGHT *'Christ Bless-*
ing the World' (c.1300-
1320). The symbolism of
the four Evangelists, fixed
signs of the zodiac and the
blessing of the world sphere
link Christianity back to our
earliest spiritual heritage.

Not only does direct zodiacal symbol-ism permeate early Christianity, but so too does numerical symbolism. The four evangelists are represented by their appro-priate animals, as I have already men-tioned, and it is significant that they are their *astrological* symbols as well: the four fixed signs, the St Mark Lion, the St Luke Bull, the St Matthew Man, and the St John Eagle. The zodiac is a circle of the animal forms of the powers of the

monthly phases of the yearly cycle. It is interesting that St John and the Virgin are the only human figures in the zodiac.

The use of four as well as twelve is commonly associated with these astrolog-ical divisions into squares and triangles. The geometrical symbolism of three, four and twelve is consistently used in a Chris-tian context, evoking its prototypical reverberation of the pre-Christian cults which also used the astrological symbols.

• • •

PARIS WEST ROSE – AN ASTROLOGICAL WINDOW

• • •

A window which illustrates the integration of astrological/cosmological images with Christian hierarchy is the West Rose at Paris, dedicated to Our Lady (Notre Dame). The twelve-fold geometry features the twelve virtues in the upper half of the outer circle, with the corresponding vices in the inner circle, while the signs of the zodiac in the inner layer below correspond to the months in the outer circle. The innermost layer of twelve contains the twelve prophets, centred around the Virgin.

The zodiac signs represent the yearly energy patterns which are integral to all sacred geometry from the siting of these cathedrals to the symbols in their rose windows, to the significance of the figures throughout the buildings. The cosmos remains a central feature of the design at every level, even past the time when its outer codes had been rejected by the Church as being 'pagan'. It is understandable that the Church saw astrology as an omnipresent threat - and still does today. However, it resolutely refuses to be dislodged from the collective psyche.

The window at Lausanne carries the zodiacal theme a step further, because it also describes the entire process of creation. Here, cosmological speculation and sacred imagery join to produce a stunning window and a statement of the medieval world view which is unparalleled, being both real and symbolic at the same time. It utilizes the theme we have found in every evidence of the sacred in architecture from the earliest creation myths - that of the square and circle. In this window all things that are earthly and temporal (bound by time) are shown within a square, while things that are

FIGURE 228 • LEFT
Lausanne Cathedral, Switzerland, (c. 1230). Detail of the rose window that depicts the Imago Mundi (Image of the World), a wonderful cosmological treatise in glass and stone. This group shows the element Water, the signs Capricorn, Aquarius and Pisces, and the Moon being drawn across the sky in a chariot.

celestial and atemporal are displayed within a circle or a part of a circle.[71]

At the centre is the Creation of the World, surrounded by the divisions of the year into four seasons and twelve months, beyond which are the twelve zodiacal signs and the four elements. The motif of four and twelve again shows the geometrical structure of creation. At the edge of the world are the four rivers of Paradise and their creatures, and outside the four winds of heaven. The composition is sublime and the final result beautiful.

Every rose window is a history of creation with the layers of symbols, the numbers of circles or images in each ring, the geometrical relationship from ring to ring, and the subject matter all contributing to describe a view of the cosmos. Paradoxically, these medieval Christian views evoke comparisons with the ideas of Plato and Plotinus, and what eventually came to be considered the pagan world. The subject matter and its form of representation is very similar to various eastern mandalas showing the creation schemes of non-Christian religions.

• • •

THE CHARTRES MAZE

• • •

In the structure of Chartres cathedral, the maze occupies a unique position because if the wall containing the North Rose window were hinged at the ground and bent down, the rose window would cover the maze exactly.[72] The higher rose window represents the Last Judgment, and the labyrinth on the ground represents the path of the human soul through the life process on earth. As Chartres was intended to be a pilgrimage church, it was fitting that the builders should place a design showing such a path on the floor of the great building. Again, the maze is also a mandala, a wheel of life along eastern lines, or a horizontal wheel of fortune. There is only one path to the centre, which requires a sequence of movements which symbolically duplicate the movements of the planets. This implies that the entire building is an initiation centre, and the path the spiritual body takes above is reflected in the more mundane path of the life below on earth. As Above, So Below. The confusion leads to a purification process which initiates the soul and frees it from the treadmill of further incarnation.

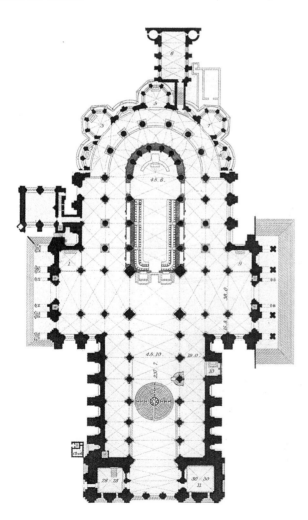

• • •
ASTRONOMICAL ABBEYS
• • •

GREY AMONG THE MEADOWS, SOLITARY, BARE:
THY WALLS DISMANTLED, AND THY RAFTERS LOW,
NAKED TO EVERY WIND AND CHILLY AIR
THAT STEEPS THE NEIGHBOURING MARSH, YET
STANDEST THOU,
GREAT CLOISTRAL MONUMENT OF OTHER DAYS!
THOUGH MARKED BY ALL THE STORMS THAT BEAT
THEE THROUGH,
A RADIANT PARABLE OF HEAVENLY WAYS.

FROM A. M. BUCKTON'S
SONGS OF JOY[73]

FIGURE 230 • LEFT
*Chartres Cathedral, Interior.
The maze is seen in the
centre of the nave.*

FIGURE 231 • BELOW
LEFT *Chartres Cathedral
Maze. The maze is a man-
dala with a rose at its centre.
The thirteenfold geometry
which determined the size of
the central flower certainly
relates to the 13 lunar months
in the year. The maze is
directly above a powerful 'tel-
luric' earth current, detectable
by dowsing, which causes
spiritual effects upon those
walking the maze.*

FIGURE 232 • BELOW
Glastonbury Abbey.

The geometry of the maze operates along similar lines to that of the rose windows. The central pattern within the maze is created by constructing a thirteen-sided star, similar to the way in which the central position of Christ is defined in the windows.

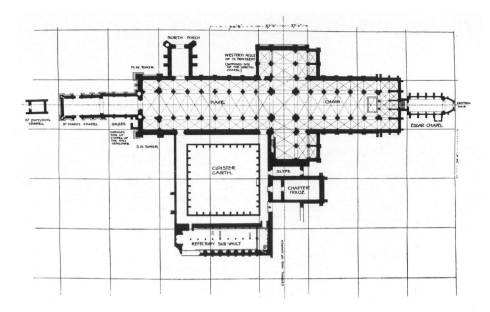

FIGURE 233 • ABOVE
Glastonbury Abbey, Plan.

FIGURE 234 • BELOW
Glastonbury Abbey, Plan of the Lady Chapel (1184 AD). The plan of the Lady Chapel lies within a hexagon and its exterior and interior proportions are both described by the vesica piscis and its measurements based on the standard British foot.

Bligh Bond was the architect in charge of the preservation and restoration of Glastonbury Abbey, which was built in the early thirteenth century. Glastonbury has a miraculous history, stretching back into the mists of Avalon, when it was a pagan holy centre sacred to the earth goddess. It was also believed to be the place to which Joseph of Arimathea travelled with the Holy Grail after the crucifixion.

As a result of Bligh Bond's investigations, it became clear that the entire com-plex of buildings was constructed on a regular grid of squares of seventy-four feet or 888 inches. St Mary's Chapel is the site of the first Christian church at Glastonbury founded by Joseph of Ari-mathea and twelve saints. The ground plan holds many of the shapes familiar to sacred architecture. The building is inscribed within a hexagon and circle with a diameter of 79.20 feet, a reference to the 7,920 miles diameter of the earth. This diameter is also the same as that of the bluestone ring at Stonehenge.

The proportions of the building itself are exactly that of a rectangle containing a vesica piscis. When a circle is inscribed within the vesica, and vesicas inscribed within it, a process identical to that seen at Stonehenge, it determines the exact size and proportion of the interior of the chapel and the position of the entrances.

• • •

MEDIEVAL ASTROLOGICAL ARCHITECTURE

• • •

After the Crusades and the building of the great cathedrals, a rash of buildings with sacred themes arose, particularly in north-ern Italy. Earlier Byzantine architecture used symbolism everywhere, possibly due to its closeness to the iconography of the

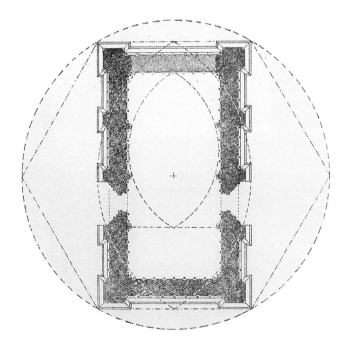

East in contrast to the stark Christianity of Europe during the Dark Ages.

Medieval Christian architecture often contains symbols derived from Roman and Greek buildings, together with earlier pagan symbols from the countryside.

The Florentine basilica of San Miniato al Monte has been studied extensively by Fred Gettings[74] because it contains a remarkable zodiac of coloured marble. The medieval mind took it for granted that the symbols should be beautiful and carry spiritual light. The symbols appear in ornament in the marble floor of the nave, in the pavement and in the nave zodiac. He found a complex of occult and theological symbols throughout the building, and believes that it is not only a huge zodiac, but a 'philosophical machine' in its action and purpose.

The power of this zodiac is accentuated by the connections it makes with the rest of the basilica. It participates in the apparent daily movement of the sun. Instead of the nave axis having an east-west alignment, as was standard with churches at the time, it is distinctly splayed to that axis. The answer to the orientation lies in the nave zodiac, which has a rayed sun at its centre, which is unusual as the earth was considered to be the centre of the solar system, and indeed the universe, at that time. At sunrise the rays enter the basilica through a side chapel and illuminate the Taurus zone of the zodiacal circle on the nave floor.

In attempting to determine why the Taurean motif was stressed when the Pisces correlation with the Virgin and Christ are usually the central concept, Gettings discovered that there was a momentous astrological event on 28 May 1207, at about the time when the floor was created. On that day the Sun, the

Moon, Mercury, Venus and Saturn were all gathered closely in the sign Taurus, an event that will not be repeated for thousands of years. It is bound up with the foundation date of the church itself, and esoteric symbolism expressing sacrifice and redemption.

In addition, on the days when the sun is in the fourth degree of Virgo and the twenty-sixth degree of Aries, its rays shine across the apse and on to the left foot of Christ. The reason for this remains obscure, but the fact is incontestable.

Gettings believes that San Miniato is central to an arcane symbolism which unites heaven and earth, and finds the core of its meaning to be astrological and solar, a unique combination of elements at the time. He links the meaning back to Egypto-Chaldean times when such solar cults were dominant and it may refer to a revision of such beliefs in medieval Italy.

FIGURE 235 • ABOVE
San Miniato, Florence, Italy (c.1190).

The Art of Memory' was developed by the Greeks as an essential part of basic education. The goddess Mnemosyne (Memory) was the mother of the Muses, and the respect accorded her demonstrates the importance the Greeks placed on an accurate and efficient memory.

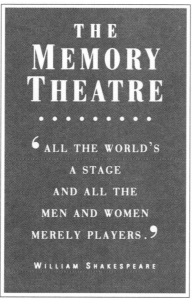

THE MEMORY THEATRE

• • • • • • • • •

6 ALL THE WORLD'S A STAGE AND ALL THE MEN AND WOMEN MERELY PLAYERS. 9

WILLIAM SHAKESPEARE

Until the invention of printing almost two thousand years later, the primary way one could gain access to information was by word of mouth. And, having heard a play or story or the recounting of a battle, the only way to store it was in the memory. There were few manuscripts to record information. The Greeks therefore created a memory art based on a technique of creating a series of 'places' and 'images' in the mind.

The art was reputed to have been invented by the poet Simonides, who chanted a poem dedicated to a Thessalian nobleman and his guests at a special occasion, but dedicated half of the poem to Castor and Pollux. As a result of the split dedication, the nobleman offered to pay Simonides only half of the agreed sum. A messenger arrived shortly afterwards requesting that Simonides step outside to see two gentlemen, and upon doing so, the roof of the banquet hall collapsed, killing the nobleman and all his guests. In the ensuing destruction and confusion, the dead were impossible to identity, but such was Simonides' memory that he was able to remember the place of every guest in the hall. This exercise gave him the idea for the art of memory.[75] It was imputed that the two gentlemen were the gods Castor and Pollux in disguise.

The essence of the art of memory is that to train the mind, one must select places and form mental images of the things one wishes to remember and store the images in those places, so that the order of the places preserves the order of the things, and the images of the things will denote the things themselves. The process is much like using a wax tablet and letters.

Roman rhetorical speakers and politicians such as Cicero used the memory art so that they could deliver long speeches with great accuracy. This tradition, established by the Greek and Roman orators, poets and actors, was carried through to the present time, although since the Renaissance and the invention of printing, rhetoric has been of minor rather than central importance.

FIGURE 236 • LEFT
The Seven Liberal Arts, by Giovanni dal Ponte (1376-1437).

FIGURE 237 • BELOW
Figure Intellectus by A T Mann. This diagram is based upon a drawing by Giordano Bruno (1533-1600) as a basis for integrating the memory art with astrology. Every day in the year is shown in its geometrically and astrologically correct place. The mandala may be used as a way of organizing the psyche and achieving spiritual integration.

ARCHITECTURAL MEMORY ARTS

The Greeks and Romans used contemporary architecture and sculpture as a foundation of the art of memory. A spacious and varied building with which the individual was very familiar was memorized, including the decorations and sculpture in the rooms. The speech to be remembered was associated with specific images, and the images were stored in a consistent and organized manner in the places within the building. When it was necessary to remember the speech, the orator would travel in his imagination through the building, retrieving the images from the places upon which he had placed them. The order was fixed by the order of the building. In this manner, very long speeches could be remembered verbatim.

The places (*loci* in Latin) should be selected with great care. Their structure and relationships are important because they are used over and over again. The places remain in the memory as the various sets of memory images come and go. There are elaborate criteria for these memory places, including their ideal distance from each other, their size, shape, illumination, colour and other configurative conditions. The buildings can also either be actual buildings or imaginary ones.

The images have similar rules to guide their selection. In the classical sources, particularly *Ad Herennium*,[76] there is a clear psychological rationale for the choice of images. Some images are remembered very clearly, while others are not so clear. The book assumes that Nature teaches the correct choice. Banal and uninteresting things make for hazy memory images, while evocative images bring memory to vivid and sharp definition. Arousing emotional effects, unusual characteristics, and bizarre forms all create good memory images. It is clear in this context that a highly valuable psychological issue is illustrated by the correct use of the memory art, and that vivid recollection is enhanced by positive emotional content and reinforcement.

THE PLATONIC MEMORY IDEA

Plato believed that there is a knowledge to which we have access which both precedes and transcends the life of our sense impressions, latent in our soul's memory. These 'Ideas' are forms of realities which the soul carries into life. In Plato's definition, true knowledge involves fitting the input from sense impressions into the imprinted higher

FIGURE 238 • BELOW
Discovering the Archetypal World. From a late 15th century German book.

reality of which physical reality is a mere reflection. Plato's implication is valuable for the study of sacred architecture because the formal systems derived from ideas are the result of remembering the true Ideas of things. All supposedly 'original' formal concepts are by definition false and superficial. The Platonic form of memory art practised in the Renaissance is organized in relation to the realities of the archetypal world.

The Platonist orators, including Cicero, brought a different and higher quality to the memory art. They modified the selection of images by introducing a moral and ethical slant to the choice. Thus the very process of memorization produced a cosmic, ethical quality to the art.

Aristotle believed memory to be the very basis of knowledge, as it is the modification of the input from the senses by memory which creates the material of intellect. It is more important to remember the relativity of the images in the mind than to remember their mere existence. Aristotle implied that it is the soul which makes higher thought processes possible, and that imagination emanates from the same part of the soul. His ideas on the processes of recollection of one's past associations, and the inherent order or disorder among the mental images which compose the rational mind, eventually came to form the foundation for the psychology of Freud and Jung.

• • •

METRODORUS AND THE ASTROLOGICAL MEMORY ART

• • •

One of the most fascinating examples of the classical memory art is that of Metrodorus of Scepsis,[77] a contemporary of Cicero. Metrodorus was a Greek man of letters who was knowledgeable in politics, culture, rhetoric and the new orientalism which penetrated the Greek world before Christ.

The memory art of Metrodorus was based on three hundred and sixty places related to degrees of the zodiacal circle. Traditional memory places were divided into groups of five and ten, so likewise Metrodorus utilized the existing divisions of the zodiac into twelve signs and thirty-six decans of ten degrees each, for each of which there was an associated decan figure. He would group sets of ten images under one more powerful image, and locate any image by its number and its decan figure.

The power of the memory system of Metrodorus was such that he could not only remember exactly what he had heard, but he could also go backwards through an evening's conversation and remember everything said. (Mind you, it would have required someone else who remembered equally well to verify it!) His system was fascinating because it meant that the order of the zodiac and its progression of known signs and decan figures could be used instead of, or together with, an architectural technique to improve further the power of memory art.

Memory training was also used for religious purposes. Many of the great teachers of the Pythagorean revival, as well as Augustine and Thomas Aquinas in late antiquity, utilized memory systems to instill Christian concepts in their students. The Jesuits still use memory as the corner stone of their religious and moral education. The rose windows of the great cathedrals also utilized such a memory system inherent in their structure, order and symbolism.

FIGURE 239 • ABOVE
Baldwin Hill Mandala by A T Mann. Such diagrams focus the mind and provide memory places for information.

FIGURE 240 • RIGHT
*Dante's Inferno by
Gustave Doré. 'Scarcely had
his feet reached to the lowest of
the bed breech, Were over us
the steep they reach'd.'
Canto XXII.*

FIGURE 241 • BELOW
*Dante's Inferno by Gustave
Doré. 'Forthwith that image
vile of Fraud appeared.'
Canto XVIII.*

FIGURE 242 • FAR RIGHT
*Vision of Hell by the Brussels
Initials Master. Images of Hell
such as this helped create
loyalty to the Church.*

ARCHITECTURAL MEMORY DEVICES

In the medieval world the principles of the memory art were often applied to buildings and the iconography within them. For a largely uneducated populace, the messages of religious stories could be easily transmitted by their art and architecture. The virtues and vices are recorded in buildings, particularly monastic and religious buildings, so that the moral and devotional qualities of the people could be educated and heightened. The outer form of the buildings reflected the inner eye of the devotional monk or peasant.

Frances Yates found memory images in medieval art and architecture, such as the paintings of Giotto in Padua, Lorenzetti's commissions in the Palazzo Communale in Siena, and the Dominican church of Santa Maria Novella in Florence where the organization of heaven and hell are represented, as well as in Dante's *Inferno* (both in the early manuscripts and in Titian's representation of it).[78] The power of images shows how immediate and effective the memory art was, and how easily it could be integrated into art, literature and architecture.

GIULIO CAMILLO'S MEMORY THEATRE

Giulio Camillo (1480-1544) was one of the most famous men of the sixteenth century because he created a memory theatre, a portable wooden theatre into which only two people could enter, which contained the keys to the mysteries of the world. The secret of how it worked and the inner form of the theatre

FIGURE 243 • BELOW
The Old Cabbalist. The Hebrew Cabala organized the letters onto the tree of life, which became a primary magical method for organizing information and the psyche as a memory system in medieval times.

was to be revealed to only one person in the world, the King of France.

It was claimed that anyone entering the magical theatre of Giulio Camillo would come out discoursing on any subject at Cicero's level of understanding. The integration of amphitheatre architecture and imagery was such that it contained memory places and loci which could contain all known knowledge. Giulio Camillo even claimed that it contained echoes of both mind and soul constructed in wood.

The power and reputation of Camillo's memory theatre was supported by the fact that he represented the emerging Hermetic philosophy of the Renaissance. From the late fifteenth century books appeared which claimed to represent the mysteries of the Egyptians, particularly the Egyptian god of knowledge and letters, Thoth Hermes Trismegistus, or the god Mercury. These writings, specifically the *Corpus Hermeticum* and the *Asclepius,* combined the mystical traditions of the

Hebrew Kabbalah with the philosophy of the Egyptians, Pythagoreans and Platonists.[79] These ideas were espoused by some of the greatest men of the time, including Marsilio Ficino, Pico della Mirandola and others. The Hermeticists believed that the mind was influenced by the quality and organization of the images stored within it by the soul and reflected the sensory input of a lifetime. By attracting superior imagery, the soul would be more likely to be fulfilled and thus attain a higher spiritual state.

• • •

ENTERING THE MEMORY THEATRE

• • •

Camillo's theatre was reconstructed by Frances Yates (see Figure 244). There are seven steps and seven gangways, representing the seven planets. The spectator looks from the stage into the audience of the amphitheatre at the people seated there. The positions and qualities of the people are the places upon which the memory system relies. Since the more important distinguished people typically sat on the lowest seats at the theatre, so in the memory theatre the closest seats are the most important and the seats become less important the further they are from the stage. The design of the theatre was apparently based upon the organization of the Greek theatre in Vitruvius' *De Architectura.*

Camillo's theatre varies from the Vitruvian model because each gangway has a gate or door decorated with many images. In Camillo's theatre the traditional function is reversed: instead of the audience occupying the seats looking at the stage, the observer stands on the stage looking out into the audience.

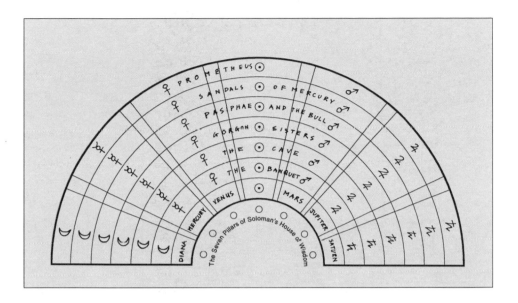

The seven-fold memory system of the theatre is based on Solomon's seven pillars of wisdom and the seven Sephiroth of the supercelestial world. Rather than placing the oratorical places on vague and frail things, this allowed the enlightened Platonist to utilize eternal places as distinct from mundane ones. The act of memory thus becomes a spiritual process in itself, bringing the soul to higher levels of awareness.

The images of Camillo's theatre are based on the seven planets and their characteristics, gods and goddesses, and qualities. Each row of seats represents a level of being: the Sephiroth; the planets; the angels; the Temple of Wisdom; subcelestial and elemental worlds; and astral influences. His theatre described the universe expanding from the First Cause through the stages of creation. The names he has given them are: the appearance of the elements on the Banquet; their mixture in the Cave; the creation of man in the image of God in the Gorgon Sisters; the union of soul and body in Pasiphae and the Bull; the

world of man's activities in the Sandals of Mercury; and the arts and sciences, religion and laws in Prometheus.[80] This progression of qualities is reminiscent of both the Old Testament creation system and the Platonist manifestation of the universe.

Each planetary level generates appropriate images, including the tranquillity of Jupiter, the anger of Mars, the melancholy of Saturn, the love of Venus, and so forth. The theatre enables the viewer to see the world from a higher state of consciousness, using superior images to allow the mind and soul to ascend to contact the supercelestial fountain of wisdom. Camillo successfully transformed the classical art of memory into an occult, magical, Hermetic art of the spirit.

Ficino believed it possible to capture the spirit of the stars, the astral currents which pour down from above, and use them for improved health and life. The celestial life of the spirit is the ultimate goal, and the theatre is one man's way to accomplish this goal.

FIGURE 244 • ABOVE
Giulio Camillo's Memory Theatre. Camillo's memory theatre was a repository of mythology organized using astrological and mnemotechnic devices. Each of the seven blocks of seats is identified with a planet/god or goddess and each of the rows back from the stage correlated with Solomon's Seven Pillars of Wisdom. The entire theatre was a memory device which could be internalized.

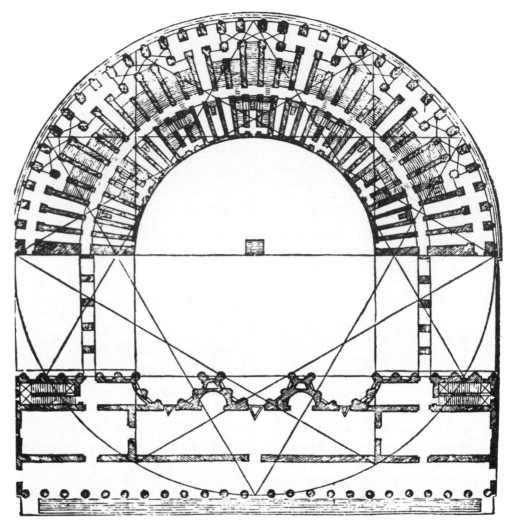

FIGURE 245 • RIGHT
Palladio's Reconstruction of the Greek Amphitheatre. Palladio's plan was derived from Daniel Barbaro's commentary on Vitruvius published in 1556. The theatre was inscribed within a circle, in which were four equilateral triangles which defined the exits, the plane of the proscenium, the size of the stage and orchestra, and other important features.

FIGURE 246 • BELOW
Theatre Masks, Perge, Turkey.

Camillo believed that his creation was a Memory Theatre of the World because it magically reflected the divine world in its proportions, architecture and imagery. The Renaissance humanist magicians had unique ideas about how the memory art could be applied to create divine powers by reflecting the macrocosm in the microcosm.

•••

TALISMANIC MEMORY IMAGES

•••

Frances Yates believed that the Renaissance mages used the memory images as inner talismans. A talisman is a diagram or image which carries magical powers, because it has been designed and made in accordance with magical rules. While they are often based on astral or astrological guidelines, their potency could be musical or visual, architectural or artistic. Many medieval doctors such as Paracelsus used talismans for healing. Objects designed with Jupiterian qualities in mind could expand, enlighten or bring good luck to their owners. Many people at that time believed that the Egyptians had mastered this art through the proportion and design of their alphabet, statues, ritual objects and architecture.

In seeking universal harmony, the Renaissance magicians developed systems of proportion based on the measurements of the human body, the microcosm, and compared them to the proportions of the planets and their orbits in the macrocosm. Celestial harmony involved their integration in such a way that the 'microcosm is the macrocosm'. Perfect proportions thus evoke magical power and the possibility of celestial harmony.

•••

THE VITRUVIAN REVIVAL

•••

Vitruvius based his description of the classical Greek theatre on the proportions of the world:

THE PLAN OF THE THEATRE ITSELF IS TO BE CONSTRUCTED AS FOLLOWS. HAVING FIXED UPON THE PRINCIPAL CENTRE, DRAW A LINE OF CIRCUMFERENCE EQUIVALENT TO WHAT IS TO BE THE PERIMETER AT THE BOTTOM, AND IN IT DESCRIBE FOUR EQUILATERAL TRIANGLES, AT EQUAL DISTANCE APART AND TOUCHING THE BOUNDARY LINE OF THE CIRCLE, AS THE ASTROLOGERS DO IN A FIGURE OF THE TWELVE SIGNS OF THE ZODIAC, WHEN THEY ARE MAKING COMPUTATIONS FROM THE MUSICAL HARMONY OF THE STARS. TAKING THAT ONE OF THESE TRIANGLES WHOSE SIDE IS NEAREST TO THE SCENA, LET THE FRONT OF THE SCENA BE DETERMINED

FIGURE 247 • ABOVE
Tree of Life by A T Mann. The tree of life was a mandala, a memory device and a philosophical model based on the structure of the universe and also of the human.

BY THE LINE WHERE THAT SIDE CUTS OFF A SEGMENT OF THE CIRCLE, AND DRAW, THROUGH THE CENTRE, A PARALLEL LINE SET OFF FROM THAT POSITION, TO SEPARATE THE PLATFORM OF THE STAGE FROM THE SPACE OF THE ORCHESTRA... THE SECTIONS FOR SPECTATORS IN THE THEATRE SHOULD BE SO DIVIDED, THAT THE ANGLES OF THE TRIANGLES WHICH RUN ABOUT THE CIRCUMFERENCE OF THE CIRCLE MAY GIVE THE DIRECTION FOR THE FLIGHTS OF STEPS BETWEEN THE SECTIONS... THE ANGLES WHICH GIVE THE DIRECTIONS FOR THE FLIGHTS OF STEPS, WILL BE SEVEN IN NUMBER; THE OTHER FIVE ANGLES WILL DETERMINE THE ARRANGEMENT OF THE SCENE: THUS, THE ANGLE IN THE MIDDLE OUGHT TO HAVE THE 'ROYAL DOOR' OPPOSITE TO IT; THE ANGLES TO THE RIGHT AND LEFT WILL DESIGNATE THE POSITION OF THE DOORS FOR GUEST CHAMBERS; AND THE TWO OUTERMOST ANGLES WILL POINT TO THE PASSAGES IN THE WINGS.[81]

The entire geometry of the theatre is composed of a series of four interlocking equilateral triangles which determine the location and positioning of all the major architectural elements. The seven gangways and gates, the entrances on the stage and the proportions of the whole evoke the magic and mystery of the creation.

• • •

PALLADIO'S TEATRO OLYMPICO

• • •

The buildings of Andrea Palladio (1550-1580) represent the psychological dynamics

FIGURE 248 • FAR RIGHT
Theatre, Ephesus, Turkey. The classical Greek theatre was set in beautiful countryside and its form was totally harmonious.

FIGURE 249 • RIGHT
San Giorgio Maggiore, Venice, Italy (begun 1565). This church by Andrea Palladio (1508-1580) is across the lagoon from Piazza San Marco in Venice.

seven gangways, the triangles also determine the positions of the five doors on to the stage.

One of Palladio's most interesting buildings is the Teatro Olympico in Vicenza. The theatre was a faithful homage to Vitruvius, whose design Palladio adapted. The stage utilized some quite magical effects, because it is banked steeply so that from the audience the streets on stage appear to vanish into the far distance. The theatre was full of symbolic objects and overrun with memory places, making it ideal for memory work.

FIGURE 250 • ABOVE
Palladian Villa in the Veneto.

FIGURE 251 • RIGHT
Teatro Olympico, Interior. This stage set designed by Vincenzo Scamozzi (1552-1616) beautifully complements the theatre designed by Palladio. Notice the streets radiating away from centre stage - Palladio exagerated their perspective by ramping them up and making the perspective shift more extreme.

of the late sixteenth century in the Veneto. His architecture expressed the qualities of openness and acknowledgment to the glorious past. All architects at this time used Vitruvius' books on architecture as their bible, and Palladio was no exception. He reconstructed the Greek theatre directly from the work of Vitruvius. The base of one triangle determines the position of the back of the stage, its opposite points into the central gangway and determines the size of the seating section. Vitruvius states that the four equilateral triangles which determine the form, proportions and organization of the theatre correspond to the *trigona* which astrologers inscribe within the circle of the zodiac. The circular form of the theatre reflects the form of the zodiac, complete with the seven gangways corresponding to the seven planets and the four triangles corresponding to the four elements, fire, air, earth and water. In addition to the

FIGURE 252 • LEFT

Teatro Olympico, Vicenza by Andrea Palladio. The stage of the Teatro Olympico as drawn by Palladio (1579-1580).

FIGURE 253 • BELOW

The Spiritual Brain by Robert Fludd. The three higher faculties of reason, intellect and mind were believed to reside in the upper part of the brain. Higher humanity has contact with the archetypal world of God above through the mind.

• • •

ROBERT FLUDD'S MEMORY THEATRE

• • •

Robert Fludd (1574-1637) was a highly controversial medical doctor and Hermeticist of the late English Renaissance. He claimed to be a Rosicrucian and his books describe a magical philosophy

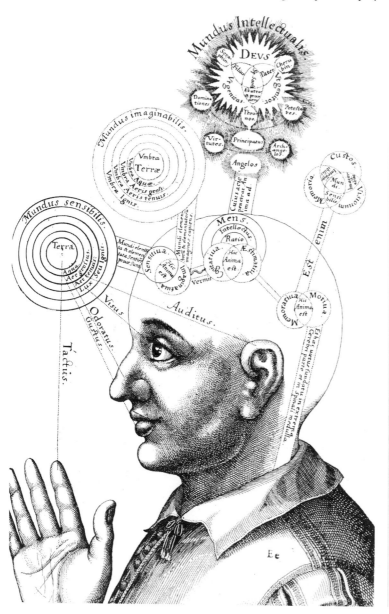

based on Egyptian ideals which are profusely illustrated to support his contentions. All of the visual material in Fludd's books, which he called hieroglyphics, show clearly that he used the concepts of the magical memory theatre as a metaphor for the world of ideas.

Fludd made a distinction between what he called the 'round art' and the 'square art' of memory.[82] The round art uses memory forms which do not exist in the physical world - such as spirits, souls, images of gods and goddesses, angels and so on - in an astrological circular pattern. This art uses magical diagrams, talismans and mandalas, all animated with celestial influences. The square art uses physical memory images such as men, animals, buildings, rooms, statues, and such like. The square art is architectural while the round art is astrological - although both carry powerful magic to improve memory and convey cosmic images. The distinction Fludd makes is that while the square art which uses real buildings is easier to use because of a natural familiarity with buildings, the round art uses imaginary places and is better adapted to an astro-

logically-based intellect because it is based on ideas.[83]

Fludd's own memory system naturally integrates the qualities of the round art and the square art. He believed that the zodiac and planetary spheres of the round art could be combined with buildings containing memory places with memory images from the square art, creating a celestial art which utilized the best of both systems, a series of cubicles and niches containing organic celestial images of gods and goddesses.

Fludd called these synthetic buildings to be placed in the heavens 'theatres', although they are in reality only stages from theatres. He wanted to make a system in which the memory places were also activated naturally by planetary movements. In his illustrations to his great work *Utriusque Cosmi... Historia*, Fludd included a diagram showing the circular zodiac upon which the round art would be based on the page opposite a stage showing his theatre of the square art. As Frances Yates pointed out, when the book was closed, the circular starry sky would have covered the theatre. The heavens work through the theatres and vice versa. This is a clue to his intentions.

Fludd displayed many variations of his memory stage complete with five stage openings and sometimes upper balconies and windows, and mentioned that he perceived the theatre as a place where comedies and tragedies could be enacted. He also implied that two theatres would be included in each zodiacal sign in his magical astrological memory system. The five stage doors are used as memory places as in the traditional art of memory, and they stand in relationship to five columns identified by different geometrical shapes such as the circle, square and

hexagon. Fludd's theatres have a profound architectural quality which leads us to the conclusion that they have a prototype in the world.

• • •

THE GLOBE THEATRE

• • •

The original Globe Theatre was erected on the south bank of the Thames in 1599 and was used until it burned down in 1613, when it was immediately rebuilt on the same foundations. The most obvious interest in the Globe is that William Shakespeare belonged to the Lord Chamberlain's company of actors who used the theatre for their performances, and he could have been involved in its foundation.

While some engravings of the Globe have survived, the theatre has been the subject of much speculation as to exactly how it was structured and designed. The best evidence of the interior of the Globe survives as the De Witt drawing

FIGURE 254 • LEFT
Robert Fludd, Paracelsian physician, philospher and occultist (1574-1637).

FIGURE 255 • TOP
The Theatre, from Robert Fludd's Ars Memoriae. *The central entrance is the place of spirit, those on either side the expressions of the soul, and the wing entrances relate to the domain of the mind.*

FIGURE 256 • ABOVE
The Theatre, from Robert Fludd's Ars Memoriae. *The theatre illustrated by Fludd shows the five main openings used in the memory art as loci, and the five imprints of column bases at the front of the stage. The theatre would have had a painted ceiling with the signs of the zodiac, making the whole a true theatre of the world.*

FIGURE 257 • RIGHT
The De Witt Sketch of the Swan Theatre, London. From the only surviving drawing of the Swan by a Dutch traveller, sent in a letter to Johannes De Witt and discovered in 1888.

London that the theatre was hexagonal without and circular within.

The reconstructions do indicate that these theatres had columns in the open courtyard which supported a covering to protect the inner part of the stage. It is known that the underside of the covering was painted with a zodiac circle and other stars representing the heavens. The paintings would not only have been accurate diagrams of the stars and their relative positions, but also representations of the spheres of the seven planets, or even something more elaborate.[84] Thus the heavens covered the dramas enacted within the Globe.

What of the parallel between Palladio's reconstruction of the Vitruvian theatre and the actual Globe? Yates proposes a diagram showing the possible integration of these two sets of ideas about the cosmic theatre (see Figure 255). The plans are roughly commensurable, but do not make particularly edifying architecture. Frances Yates believed that the integration of Vitruvian zodiacal triangles and Fludd's symbolic geometry was a more stable guide to the basic plan of the Globe than previous reconstructions.[85]

The combination of square and circle relates the Shakespearean theatre to the original conception of the sacred temple. The Elizabethan 'theatre of the world' echoed the Leonardo man in the circle as the key to humanist Renaissance tradition, and a reflection of the relationship between macrocosm and microcosm. When created with these ideas in mind, the theatre truly represents the synthesis between the players and audience in a setting which expresses the hierarchy of spiritual levels as sacred architecture.

Fludd also mentions that the World Theatre was sited in relation to the points

(see Figure 257) which is little more than a sketch of the similar Swan Theatre. The most important, but controversial, question is whether the Globe was circular or polygonal. Maps of the time indicate its position but not its exact shape.

The exact layout of these theatres is subject to much speculation from two sources - one from architects and archaeologists and the other from researchers into the stage directions and allusions in dramatic texts of the time. It is well known that the plays of Shakespeare and his contemporaries lacked any stage directions. These were left to the directors and actors. Scholars have never been sure how locations on stage, entrance directions or other crucial directions were indicated. It is indeed possible that some of the Fludd theatre reconstructions are stage sets which would have been erected within the theatre.

The shape of the Globe was probably a combination of the three shapes Fludd uses for imaginary columns in his diagrams: the circle, the hexagon and the square, based on the recorded observation of a resident in mid-eighteenth century

of the compass, and these are marked on his engravings. The stage was at the east end of the theatre, similar in its orientation to the position of the altar in churches and cathedrals.

It is entirely possible, given the known spiritual qualities of Shakespeare's plays, that the theatre was a vehicle through which to reinforce his higher ideas. The multi-levelled openings on the stage could have signified the emergence of higher qualities. The heavens above would have represented the Platonic 'world of ideas', from which everything emanates, the middle zone of the balconies would then have been intermediary to the reality on the ground. Scenes such as the balcony scene in *Romeo and Juliet*, the death of Cleopatra in *Antony and Cleopatra*, and the death of Caliban in *Othello* show the intercourse between sacred and mundane.

• • •
A PROPOSED RECONSTRUCTION OF THE VITRUVIAN MEMORY THEATRE
• • •

Given an understanding of astrology and architecture, a stimulating alternative reconstruction of the traditional Shakespearean theatre emerges.

Two intriguing points mentioned by Frances Yates help solve the puzzle. In the classical Greek theatre where the memory art was first used, the process worked in two ways. The audience used the stage as a site for memory places for remembering the plays, and the actors used the seating of the audience as memory places for their lines. In the reconstruction it makes perfect sense to understand the theatre as a two-way process.

When the four equilateral triangles of Vitruvius are placed within the circle and form of the theatre, they determine the location of the seven gangways, which define six sections of seats. If the sections are each divided into two halves, each accessible by a gangway, it allows the placement of the twelve signs of the zodiac around the periphery of the seating so that each section has its own sign.

In Greek theatres the semicircular orchestra was where the important individuals sat during performances. In our scheme, it contains the seven planetary spheres, within which the archetypal individuals who represent the planets would be seated. When seven concentric rings are placed in the orchestra, the innermost ring of the Sun is the King, followed by the next circle for the Moon: the Queen and her ladies.

FIGURE 258• LEFT
The Globe Theatre, London (1616).
The Globe Theatre was opened in 1599 and burned down in 1616. This engraving is by Cornelius de Visscher (1619 or 1629-1662).

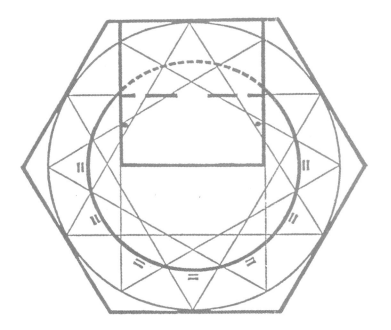

FIGURE 259 • ABOVE
*Vitruvius' Reconstruction of
the Greek Theatre.*

FIGURE 260 • ABOVE
RIGHT *Roman Theatre
Step, Side, Turkey.*

Following this would have been Mercury as the wise men or advisors; Venus as the women of court, artists, artisans and musicians; Mars as generals and military men of consequence; Jupiter as the philosophers or churchmen; and Saturn as bankers and the wealthy. Thus the planetary rings in the orchestra contain the archetypes of the planets.

The audience itself is structured similarly, with seven concentric planetary circles stepping back to form the galleries, providing seating for the populace. The first rows would be for important people associated with the Sun; the Moon ring for the important women and beautiful courtesans; and the remainder of the rings serving their purpose in an appropriate astrological order.

The combination of the radiating seating zones of the twelve astrological signs and the rings of the seven planets produces eighty-four permutations - every planet in each zodiac sign. In traditional astrology the planets in the signs of the zodiac describe all the archetypal actions of human behaviour.

• • •

MEMORY AND
STAGE DIRECTIONS

• • •

It is the organization of the stage which is most interesting. The information made available by subdividing the stage into planetary zones creates intriguing implications for the staging of Shakespearean theatre.

The shape of the stage in the Palladian reconstruction is a double square, the mystical and sacred shape traced back to the creation myths of ancient people. The marble tiles on the floor of each square are organized into seven rows and columns, making forty-nine squares in each half, or ninety-eight squares in all. The square tiles are in a black and white checker-board pattern, a common symbol for the physical universe in Masonic and Rosicrucian ritual spaces. The checker-board pattern reflects the binary quality of the universe and its laws, and is a fitting representation of the world. In tarot cards the checker-board pattern is used to sig-

FIGURE 261 • LEFT
Juno and Mars by
Giovanni Battista Carlone
(1592-1677).

nify the physical world, either as an endless landscape on the ground in the High Priest card or elevated to a higher plane, as in the Magician card.[86]

Each row of squares stepping back from the front of the stage is dedicated to a planet, from the Sun across row one to Saturn at the back across row seven. Each column stepping from right and left away from the central file is identified with one of the planets from the Sun to Saturn. Because of the checkerboard pattern, each pair of planets has both a black and white square representing their positive (white) and negative (black) astrological aspects. Astrological aspects are combinations of planets, such as Sun/Moon, Sun/Mercury, Mars/Jupiter, and so forth, and indicate the archetypal behaviourial qualities.

The grid of planetary aspects is the key to determining stage directions for plays. Shakespearean plays have always been difficult to reconstruct because no stage directions are given in their text. But he would have been familiar with the arrangement of spaces, entrances and other settings common in the public theatres in London, of which the Globe was the most perfect example. Understanding that the arrangement was archetypal, he would have had this organization in mind while he wrote his plays and assumed them to be produced

FIGURE 262 • LEFT
Theatre, Troy, Turkey.

FIGURE 263 • RIGHT
Hamlet 'Alas, poor Yorick!' from Hamlet *by William Shakespeare.*

in such theatres. And since the essence of the Shakespearean drama, like the ancient theatre, is the playing out of the destinies of humanity in a cosmic and religious setting, it would seem natural that he would have utilized the memory theatre qualities had he known of them.

If the cosmic qualities of Shakespearean drama are important as I believe them to be, the proposed reconstruction of the theatre could be used as a model for the staging of plays reflecting the Renaissance humanist perspective and would also solve the problems created by staging such plays in our time.

• • •

CREATING A
THEATRE OF THE MIND

• • •

An example of the way in which the stage could have been used to determine the positions and movements of actors is easy to illustrate.

The five entrances to the stage at ground level and the three above all have obvious meanings when considered from the cosmic perspective. The central entrance signifies the spirit, and an actor entering from this position would immediately be known as a central character speaking from a spiritual perspective. If a character left through this position, it would have signified that his or her action terminated in a spiritual quality. The entrances to either side of the centre represent the emotions - to the left negative emotions and to the right positive emotions. Thus a character emerging from left rear stage would be seen to describe negativity and a black emotional state, while if he emerged from this opening but left through the right-hand one, there would have been a transformation

from negative to positive emotion during his time on stage.

The openings to the sides of the stage represent mental states, again with left being negative or unconscious ideas or

thoughts, and right being positive or conscious ideas or thoughts. The permutations of entrances and exits could indicate to the audience the exact role of each character and clearly define their movements and states of mind.

Once on the stage, the exact position of each actor would have a precise meaning. The closer the position to the sun row across the front, or to the central file up centre stage, the greater their significance in the drama. Movement during dialogue could be choreographed to indicate to the audience the qualities expressed by each role. The staging would also represent each character and dialogue in astrological-cosmic terms.

As an example, I would like to use the opening of the famous soliloquy from *Hamlet* to illustrate Hamlet's position and movements for each line.

To be, (SUN-SUN +)

or not to be; (SUN-SUN -)

that is the question: (MERCURY-MERCURY +)

FIGURE 264 • LEFT
*Hamlet Sees the
Ghost of His Father
From* Hamlet, *by William
Shakespeare.*

Whether 'tis nobler in the mind to suffer
(JUPITER–MERCURY -)
The slings and arrows of outrageous fortune
(MARS–JUPITER -)
Or to take arms against a sea of troubles,
(MARS–SATURN -)
And by opposing end them? (SATURN–SATURN -)
To die: (MARS–SATURN -)
To sleep; (MOON–MOON +)
To sleep: perchance to dream: (MOON–MOON +)
Ay, there's the rub; (MOON–SATURN -)
*For in that sleep of death what dreams may
come* (MOON–SATURN +)
When we have shuffled off this mortal coil,
(MOON–MARS)
Must give us pause. (MERCURY–SATURN +)

A Shakespearean play choreographed
using the Astrological Memory Theatre
would synchronize the cosmic message of
the play with its underlying astrological
structure, and would be a cosmic exercise
for those who understood the language of
the theatre of the world.

Then our play's begun
When we are borne, and to the world
        first enter,
And all finde exits when their parts are done.
If then the world a theatre present,
As by the roundnesse it appears most fit,
Built with starre galleries of hye ascent,
In which Johove doth as spectator sit,
And chiefe determiner to applaud the best,
And their endeavours crowne with more
        then merit;
But by their evil actions doomes the rest
To end distrac't, whilst others praise inherit;
He that denyes then theatres should be,
He may as well deny a world to me.[87]

HUMANISM AND THE DISENCHANTMENT OF MODERNISM

• • • • • • • • •

'MODERN BUILDINGS PRESENT AN INVERSION OF THE NORMAL RELATIONSHIP BETWEEN ESSENTIAL FORMS AND CONTINGENT FORMS.'

TITUS BURCKHARDT,
SACRED ART EAST AND WEST

The Renaissance 'Age of Humanism' saw the birth of a new dimension of the spirit, and the ascendancy of architecture as an individual pursuit, which created great buildings but was the beginning of the end of the sacred tradition in architecture. Before this time buildings had been designed by guilds of master masons, as in the cathedrals, but this now changed.

Symbolic of this time is the image of the man within the circle drawn by Leonardo da Vinci. Throughout the medieval age religion had exerted a strong hold over the people, but with the influence of the Renaissance the hold began to weaken, and with it the tradition of sacred architecture. While magical and humanist images dominated the time, and wonderful architecture was designed by Brunelleschi, Bramante, Palladio, Leonardo and Michelangelo, the ancient traditions were breaking down.

Michelangelo's initial drawings of the Basilica of St Peter in Rome show an immense symmetrical cross-shaped building of great purity and beauty. The back of St Peter's still reflects these designs, but the façade and famous colonnade by Bernini are later additions.

FIGURE 265 • FAR LEFT
Old Sacristy of San Lorenzo, Florence, by Brunelleschi (1377-1446). The buildings of Florence demonstrate the beauty and elegance of classical geometry allied with humanistic spirit.

FIGURE 266 • ABOVE
The original plan for St Peter's in Rome was made in 1546 by Michelangelo.

FIGURE 267 • ABOVE
Michelangelo Buonarotti (1475-1564).

FIGURE 268 • LEFT
St Peter's Basilica, Rome. The light pouring into the basilica through the cupola is astonishing in its purity.

FIGURE 269 • ABOVE
Dr John Dee, astrologer, mathematician and philosopher (1527-1608).

FIGURE 270 • RIGHT
Giordano Bruno, astronomer, philosopher and mystic (1543-1600).

The scale of the main basilica of the Roman Church is massive and reflects the reality that the Church itself had broken away from the influence of the cosmos. This feeling was supported by the magicians, alchemists and astrologers who became custodians of the ancient Hermetic tradition. Giordano Bruno, Robert Fludd, John Dee and others carried the ideas of the past in open opposition to the Church. It is at this time that the tradition of sacred architecture disappeared.

It is curious but appropriate that the decline of sacred architecture coincided with the decline of astrology. During the late flowering of both pursuits in the sixteenth century, the sacred traditions in all areas of human endeavour were forced into hiding. Symbolic of this was the trial and condemnation of Galileo, and death of Giordano Bruno at the stake in Rome in 1600. Both espoused a sun-centred solar system, and paid the price the Roman Church demanded for such heresy. The conflict between science and spirituality had begun.

• • •

ASTROLOGY AS A REVOLUTIONARY SCIENCE

• • •

The astrologer Robert Hand has written a fascinating essay called *'Astrology as a Revolutionary Science'*,[88] in which he describes religion as a principle by which one deals with day-to-day reality and views the nature of God. To him religion is therefore a combination of metaphysics, ontology, epistemology, moral code, behaviourial standards and a reality system, which has mythological characteristics, but is not mythological in its expression.

With the dawning of the scientific era in the seventeenth century, the view of history changed dramatically. Previously there had been a romanticism about the past, particularly about the classical age of Greece and Rome in the West, or of Egyptian or Chinese empires in the Near and Far East. The new vision of the past postulated that prior civilizations and cultures were inferior or primitive. The rise of the cult of the individual was beginning to develop, and over the next three centuries it supplanted previous predominant religious beliefs.

Hand classifies religions as either Type I or Type II. Type I religions include Hinduism, Buddhism, Taoism, Hermeticism, Neoplatonism, Sufism, Kabbalism and Quakerism, and he includes mystical religions in this category. Type I religions accept:

- CYCLICAL TIME;
- THE LACK OF A CLEAR BOUNDARY BETWEEN SELF AND NOT-SELF;
- THE NEED FOR DIRECT PERSONAL EXPERIENCE OF THE DIVINE, AS THROUGH YOGA AND MEDITATION;
- A DIFFUSION OF CONSCIOUSNESS AND SPIRIT BEYOND ONE GOD;
- POLYTHEISM;
- THE CONCEPTION OF NATURE AS AN ALLY, RATHER THAN AS A PRIMITIVE FORCE TO BE DOMINATED OR PERCEIVED AS A MACHINE;
- THE ACCEPTANCE OF THE WHEEL OF REALITY, IMPLYING REINCARNATION, LIBERATION, ENLIGHTENMENT AND NIRVANA.[89]

The first Type II religions came into being about 500 BC, taught by the prophet Zoroaster. Zoroastrianism was the first religion to persecute purely on doctrinal grounds. At this time in the eastern Mediterranean a tribe of primitive monolatrists existed, worshipping one god to the exclusion of all others. These Judeans came into contact with the Persians, who had an advanced Type I system of star worship involving astrology and number mysticism. The Jews liked the ideas, but also despised them as being against their very protective and jealous God. When they were captured by the Persians, they were forced to assimilate their religious beliefs in order to survive. When some of them were allowed to return and rebuild Jerusalem, their resultant fusion of Jehovah and Ahura-Mazda led to the creation of the three monotheistic Abramic religions – Judaism, Christianity and Islam.

Thus the Type II religions were born. Their beliefs included:

- A UNIQUE CREATION WHICH OCCURS ONCE;
- LINEAR TIME;
- SELF AND NOT-SELF ARE SEPARATE AND

FIGURE 271 • ABOVE
The Parthenon, Athens.

FIGURE 272 • BELOW
Galileo Galilei, astronomer and astrologer (1564-1642).

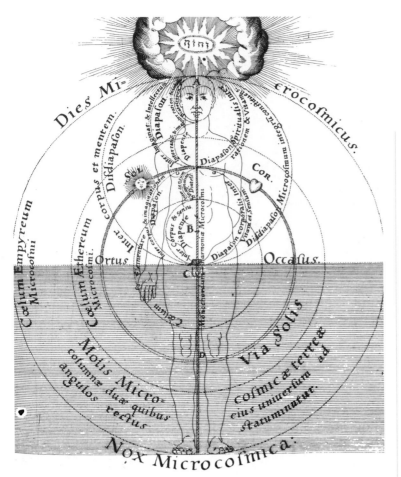

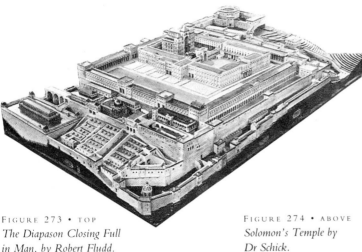

FIGURE 273 • TOP
*The Diapason Closing Full
in Man, by Robert Fludd.
The human body is composed
of the four elements vivified
by the soul. The wonderful
harmony of the elements is
brought together by the
Spiritus Mundi, shown here
as a vertical line. On it are
indicated the stages of the
soul's ascent from body
to spirit.*

FIGURE 274 • ABOVE
*Solomon's Temple by
Dr Schick.*

NOT MYSTICAL;

• THERE IS ONLY ONE REALITY AND
  DEVIATION EQUALS EVIL;

• GOD IS EXTERNAL TO THE SELF;

• THERE IS NO DIFFUSION OF
  CONSCIOUSNESS AND SPIRIT, THEY ARE
  ONLY FOUND IN GOD AND HIS ANGELS;

• MATTER AND NATURE ARE DEAD AND
  SHOULD BE CONQUERED;

• PARADISE IS A DEFINITE TIME AND PLACE
  AT SOME POINT IN THE FUTURE.

These characteristics of Type II religions can be recognised as those which became totally dominant after AD 1500.

Whereas sacred architecture comes from a Type I belief in the logos, in a mystical and symbolic view of the universe, as the Church became politically stronger, the Type II characteristics began to perceive Type I qualities as a threat punishable by death or mutilation. Type II religions define God as masculine, discourage the development of individuality, suppress alternative views, believe in the primitivity of the past, and support jealous gods. In Puritanism and Calvinism, the deity is the ultimate ego and irrevocably separate and distinct from the individual.

In the Middle Ages, practitioners of Type I religions were considered pagan devil worshippers, to be feared and destroyed. The natural qualities contained in the Type II religions were gradually eliminated, and the purity of belief became greater. Anyone accepting the existence of the life energy or symbols expressing such concepts was regarded as a heretic, and punished.

In the late Renaissance a mechanist philosophy began to form within Christianity which was a logical outgrowth of the distance established between humanity and God. Matter was explained as dead,

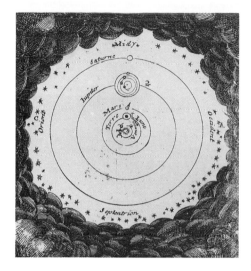

inert, and subject to mechanical laws which could be described by mathematical formulae, and nature was considered as a machine. Initially this was simply an idea, but it rapidly became a way to try to explain all nature. Descartes promulgated a natural philosophy to explain nature in direct terms, backed up by fine mathematics. Newton, the most brilliant thinker and scientist of his age, spent much time studying alchemy. For this he was attacked and forced to accept the mechanist-materialist reality. Science took its rightful place as the primary Type II religion.

Science divorces people from the direct experience of reality and teaches them to deny the self. What cannot be seen cannot exist. What cannot be measured with a ruler cannot be evaluated. Abstract ideas do not exist unless they can be objectively proven through repeatable experiments. The laws of nature are absolute and remain the same forever, without changing. Everything and everywhere in the universe is uniform. The universe is not alive in any event, therefore humanity remains separate and isolated forever.

Science has created a monstrous society. As Hand states:

FROM THIS HAS ARISEN A CULT OF THE EXPERT: THE CHILD PSYCHOLOGIST WHO HAS NEVER BEEN A PARENT, THE ANTHROPOLOGIST WHO MAKES NO EFFORT TO GET INTO THE EXPERIENCE OF CULTURAL MORES FOR FEAR THAT IT WOULD CLOUD HIS 'OBJECTIVITY'. IN MANY CASES, DIRECT, PERSONAL EXPERIENCE COUNTS AS A DISQUALIFICATION FOR EXPERTISE.[90]

We could add: the architect who has no interest in or understanding of the sacred.

Astrology is a remnant of the Type I world view that every human participates in the workings of the cosmos, rather than being a victim of it. This world view considers that every human carries psychological archetypes and has access to the collective unconscious, and the planets and signs of astrology are archetypes which act like living entities. The mystical principle that the universe is alive and in constant communication with the individual is central to the ideas of astrology. Hand is a revolutionary in that he suggests that supporting astrology is a conscious attempt to overthrow the mechanist-materialist world view which is killing life on our planet Earth. God bless him.

FIGURE 275 • TOP LEFT
The Universe According to Descartes. The system of the universe according to Descartes from the book, Description de l'Univers, contenant les Differents Systemes du Monde etc. *by Alain Manessan Mallet, published 1689.*

FIGURE 276 • ABOVE
René Descartes, philosopher (1596-1650).

FIGURE 277 • LEFT
Isaac Newton, philosopher, mathematician, astronomer and alchemist (1642-1727).

FIGURE 278 • ABOVE
Fruits of Anthroposophy
*by Rudolf Steiner. The cover
has an illustration of the
Goetheanum, designed by
Steiner and destroyed by
the Nazis.*

FIGURE 279 • TOP
RIGHT *Rudolf Steiner,
philosopher and anthro-
posophist (1861-1925).*

FIGURE 279 • FAR
RIGHT *The Second
Goetheanum by Steiner.*

• • •

THE ORGANIC
ARCHITECTURE OF
RUDOLF STEINER

• • •

Rudolf Steiner (1861-1925) founded the Anthroposophical movement earlier this century and was an architect who, while not basing his designs strictly upon the tradition of sacred architecture, did design according to rules governing the principles inherent in nature.

In 1913 Steiner designed the *Goetheanum* in Switzerland, based on Goethe's theories of organic growth. The shapes, their interrelationships, the materials and forms were derived from the metamorphosis of plants and animals. As he also created and practised a therapy featuring control of voice, which he called *eurythmy*, the building is also acoustically brilliant.

Steiner's philosophy was that all aspects of human development reflected natural patterns and that science should derive from nature. His philosophy was applied to organic gardening, diet and nutrition, and he was a forerunner of the ecological movement because he felt that humanity had a responsibility to participate in and enliven the environment rather than impose controls upon it. The ideas of his movement echo the eternal contrast between the rectangular and square realities of the physical world and the circular and spherical wholeness

FIGURE 281 • RIGHT
The Goetheanum by Steiner.

FIGURE 282 • BELOW
The Goetheanum.
Detail of a Window.

FIGURE 283 • RIGHT
The Goetheanum, Interior.
Steiner practised an organic
architecture using vegetation
as a guide to the forms
of buildings.

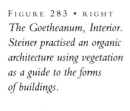

of heaven – he sought the balanced state in which both aspects of reality could be integrated.

Steiner also believed that the energetic aspect of building siting was important and that the shapes of buildings should blend into the landscape. He believed that the form-creating principles of the earth are derived from the Spirits of Form, beings of a spiritual hierarchy who are involved in the evolution of the universe and of humanity. In the beginning these spirits impressed their principles of form on humanity in the physical body, and as the races developed their unique characteristics, so their architecture reflected their level of spiritual awareness. This inherent form sense has become inbred and instinctive. Steiner felt that at the present time humanity has been left freer to withdraw from the dependence upon function and that we are coming of age. Alignment with the Spirits of Form brings elevation and an opening of consciousness, which is the true function of architecture.

• • •
MODERN ARCHITECTURE –
THE PURSUIT OF STYLE
• • •

Science attended the death of the sacred in architecture as it did in other areas of human endeavour. The effect this has had on architecture cannot be underestimated. The vacuity and deadness of modern International Style architecture and its Post-Modern successors supports this most clearly. The conspicuous absence of essence, and the elimination of the sacred in any form is the achievement of twentieth-century architecture.

It is not paradoxical that the idol of modern architects, the god I was forced to pay obeisance to in university, Le Corbusier, met his death by drowning. When I was at the Cornell University School of Architecture in the 1960s, Corbusier was god. If you did not accept this, you failed.

We all owned Le Corbusier's complete works from 1900 to his death in the 1960s. What we all found puzzling was the fact that up until the Second World War Le Corbusier had an active partnership with his cousin Pierre Jeanneret, but suddenly their partnership lapsed, without explanation. At the time it was a minor paradox, but years later the reason why became clear.

Pierre Jeanneret was a member of the French Resistance and the reason why he and his cousin split was that Le Corbusier was a virulent pro-Nazi. He made secret proposals to Hitler during the war to rebuild France, if not to rebuild Europe as the primary architect of the Third Reich. He would have worked with Albert Speer. As Le Corbusier had always wanted to raze Paris to the ground to build his *Unité d'Habitation* buildings, this supported his ideal. If he had had his way, the

FIGURE 284 • LEFT
Frank Lloyd Wright (1867-1959). The great American architect on the steps of the Capitol in Washington after appearing before the House Military Sub-committee. He urged the group to postpone the construction of a new Air Force Academy, calling its design, '...half-baked... commercial... utterly without soul or spirit!'

FIGURE 285 • BELOW
Fallingwater, Bear Run, Pennslyvania. Frank Lloyd Wright's masterpiece is integrated into nature, yet it also demonstrates a higher yearning.

FIGURE 286 • TOP RIGHT *Le Corbusier, or Charles-Edouard Jeanneret, (1887-1965), architect.*

FIGURE 287 • FAR RIGHT *The pilgrimage Chapel of Notre Dame du Haut, Ronchamp, France, is one of the more organic and effective of Le Corbusier's buildings, reflecting his interest in and practice of cubist painting.*

entire face of western society would be more monstrous than even Prince Charles could imagine.

• • •

THE VACUUM OF MODERN ARCHITECTURE

• • •

Modern architecture since Le Corbusier has been tedious and inhuman. The American architect Frank Lloyd Wright (1867-1959) was virtually the only ray of light. He was supported by his last wife Olgivanna, who was a disciple of the Russian mystic and sage George Gurdjieff, and accepted the mystical view of the sacred. Unfortunately, he was unable, except in rare cases, to gain commissions for buildings larger than houses.

Architecture today is eclectic and uninteresting. There are those architects who write about sacred geometry, but unfortunately they seem to lack any design skills to turn the tide to significance. Architecture is in a terminal state of decline.

• • •

THE FUTURE OF THE SACRED

• • •

FIGURE 288 • BELOW *Detail of the chapel of Notre Dame du Haut at Ronchamp.*

The widespread dissatisfaction with modern architecture is symbolic of the unhappiness of people with what we have done to our beautiful earth. We have systematically raped and plundered the earth and lost respect for our heritage, physically and spiritually. But now is the time to reclaim this heritage.

The increasing awareness of ecology has led to a revitalization of many of the ways of understanding the universe which previously would have been the domain of the sacred. Indeed, sacred geometry and related pursuits are becoming an increasingly broad field of interest for many aware people. What is now required is a 'new human ecology'.

We cannot continue accepting architectural design from architects who are totally divorced from a sensitivity to the world and the sacred. The great architects of this century, almost without exception, have chosen to live in buildings built before they were born, designed by anonymous architects or builders in an age when quality and integrity still reigned. This says something profound about the state of the modern movement. Post-Modernism is only another style, another disguise, another changing of the King's New Clothes. Sir Norman Foster's gesture to Feng Shui in the design of the Hong Kong and Shanghai Bank is exactly that and no more. There is little evidence of a genuine desire for a new architecture appropriate to the intense needs of our troubled times.

The New Sacred Architecture begins with new architects. Only when architectural students are taught the mysteries, the magic of symbolism, astrology and mythology made real, and the reality of the sacred, will a new architecture arise, like a phoenix, from the ashes all around us.

REFERENCES

• • •

1. See A. T. Mann, *The Round Art: The Astrology of Time and Space, Life Time Astrology*, and *The Divine Plot: Astrology and Reincarnation*.

2. Titus Burckhardt, *Sacred Art in East and West*, pp 7-8 and John Anthony West, *Serpent in the Sky*.

3. Burckhardt, p 8

4. William Stirling, *The Canon, An Exposition of the Pagan Mystery Perpetuated in the Cabala as the Rule of All the Arts*, p. xi.

5. According to Schwaller de Lubicz, 618 (0-1) lunation cycles of 29.53 days (modern astronomers reckon a lunation as 29.53059 days) is equivalent to 50 years. (618 x 29.53 = 18249 days, and 50 x 365 = 18250 days, a difference of 1 day in 50 years.) See John Anthony West, *Serpent in the Sky*, p 106.

6. Pythagoras was a Greek philosopher and initiate of the Egyptian, Babylonian, Chaldean and Mosaic mysteries, who taught that number was the foundation of all knowledge.

7. Marie-Louise von Franz, *Number and Time*, p 74.

8. Johannes Kepler (1571-1630), was a German scientist who discovered the mathematics of the planetary orbits, originally through a revelation from God. He believed that they must be circular, because any other form would have been unworthy.

9. For attributions and other correspondences of letters to numbers, astrological signs and planets, qualities and many other symbolic languages, see Aleister Crowley, *The Kabbalah of Aleister Crowley*, pp 1-40, and also S. L. MacGregor Mathers, *The Kabbalah Unveiled*, and I. Myer, *Qabbalah: The Writings of Avicebron*. There are many versions of the correspondences from all ages, few of which agree in detail, but all of which agree in principle.

10. See F. Bligh Bond, *Gematria*.

11. See Crowley, *The Kabbalah of Aleister Crowley*; von Franz, *Number and Time*; MacGregor Mathers, *The Kabbalah Unveiled*; and Jeff Love, *The Quantum Gods*.

12. H. E. Huntley, *The Divine Proportion*, p 54.

13. Translation of Akkadian Myths and Epics by E. A. Speiser in Santillana and von Dechend, *Hamlet's Mill*, p 430.

14. Santillana and von Dechend, *Hamlet's Mill*.

15. See A. T. Mann, *The Divine Plot: Astrology and Reincarnation*, p 25.

16. Ibid, and illustrations between pp 162-3.

17. William Lethaby, *Architecture, Mysticism and Myth*, p 44.

18. See the books of Schwaller de Lubicz, particularly *Sacred Science*, pp 88-94, where he presents the concept that the entire Egyptian religion is derived from and represents astronomical and nature myths.

19. Lethaby, p 15 and Jung, *Man and His Symbols*, p 133.

20. Lethaby, p 35.

21. Burckhardt, pp 27-30.

22. Ibid, p 29.

23. *Sacred Books of the East*, mentioned in Burckhardt, p 45.

24. Dr E. C. Krupp, *Echoes of Ancient Skies*, pp 205-8.

25. The Hermetic tradition was a humanist philosophy interlaced with influences from Platonism, Stoicism, Jewish mysticism, Gnosticism, magic, astrology and oriental religions. Although reputed to have started in Egypt with the god Hermes, its primary literature dates back to Greek and Roman times. It is properly a religion, a cult without temples, followed in the mind alone, which became popular during the Renaissance revival of Egyptian and other ancient forms of magical thought. For fascinating information see the books of Frances Yates, particularly *Giordano Bruno and the Hermetic Tradition*.

26. John Michell, *The City of Revelation*, p 26.

27. Ibid, pp 64-5.

28. Robert Temple, *The Sirius Mystery*.

29. Ibid, pp 127-49.

30. See Martin Brennan, *The Boyne Valley Vision*, and *The Stars and the Stones*.

31. Brennan, *The Stars and the Stones*, p. 10.

32. Ibid, p. 20.

33. Ibid, pp 158-9.

34. Lockyer (1836-1920) postulated the existence of a gas with the properties of helium twenty-seven

years before helium was found on earth, and was a pioneer of the astronomical orientation of megalithic monuments and pyramids.

35. Michell, *The City of Revelation*, p 55.

36. Michell, *The View Over Atlantis*, p xxvii.

37. Gerald Hawkins and John White, *Stonehenge Decoded*, p 47.

38. Michael Saunders, 'Stonehenge Planetarium', pp 17-18.

39. Evan Hadingham, *Early Man and the Cosmos*, p 181.

40. Ibid.

41. Burckhardt, p 23-4.

42. Ibid, p 24.

43. Ibid, p 33.

44. The Great Mother is often called Yin-Yang before the separation into separate qualities, expressed in the figure of Nu Gua, a divine being who brought civilization and order to China after the Great Flood. She rules over both Heaven and Earth, and is associated with the constellation of the Great Bear. For further study see Colegrave, *The Spirit of the Valley*, pp 31-4.

45. Stephen Skinner, *The Living Earth Manual of Feng-Shui*, p 39.

46. Sarah Rossbach, *Feng Shui*, pp 68-9.

47. Michell, *The View Over Atlantis*, p 57.

48. Ibid, p 131.

49. See Guy Underwood, *The Pattern of the Past*.

50. Herbert Weaver, *Divining the Primary Sense*, pp 40-1.

51. See C. G. Jung, *Word and Image*.

52. Giuseppe Tucci, *The Theory and Practice of the Mandala*.

53. Stirling, *The Canon*, p 31.

54. Patrick Nuttgens, *The Story of Architecture*, p 32.

55. For a biography of Schwaller de Lubicz, see André Vandenbroeck, *Al-Kemi: A Memoir*, and for a presentation of his work see John Anthony West, *Serpent in the Sky*, as well as his own books listed in the bibliography.

56. West, p 10.

57. Ibid, p 51.

58. Ibid, p 64.

59. Ibid, pp 175-6.

60. Peter Dawkins, *Arcadia*, p 39.

61. Schwaller de Lubicz, *Sacred Science*, p 281.

62. D. Davidson and H. Aldersmith, *The Great Pyramid: Its Divine Message*, p v.

63. Ibid, p 490.

64. Seyyed Hussein Nasr, *Islamic Science*, p 28.

65. Painton Cowen, *Rose Windows*, p 7.

66. Ibid, p 14.

67. Ibid, p 43.

68. Ibid, p 34.

69. Ibid, pp 122-3.

70. Ibid, p 125.

71. Ibid, p 129.

72. Critchlow, Keith, 'Chartres Maze' p 11-21.

73. Poem by A. M. Buckton, from his *Songs of Joy*, from Bligh Bond, p xi.

74. See Fred Gettings, *The Secret Zodiac: The Hidden Art in Medieval Astrology*.

75. The story of Simonides and the inspiration and information for this section is derived from the marvellous books by Frances Yates, *The Art of Memory*, and *Giordano Bruno and the Hermetic Tradition*.

76. Frances Yates, *The Art of Memory*, p 27.

77. Ibid, p 52.

78. For the connection between Dante's *Divine Comedy* and the symbolism of the tarot, see Joseph Campbell and Richard Roberts, *Tarot Revelations*.

79. Ibid, p 140.

80. Ibid, p 145.

81. Yates, *The Art of Memory*, pp 114-5, quoted from Vitruvius, *De architectura*, V, 6, i-iii.

82. I named my major work on astrology *The Round Art* after this idea of Fludd's.

83. Yates, *The Art of Memory*. p 316

84. Ibid, p 332.

85. Ibid, p 346.

86. See the symbolism of tarot as architectural landscapes in Mann, *The Mandala Astrological Tarot*.

87. Thomas Heywood, *An Apology for Actors*, London, 1612 (Shakespeare Society Reprint, London, 1841, p 13.)

88. Robert Hand, 'Astrology as a Revolutionary Science' in Mann, et al, *The Future of Astrology*.

89. Ibid, p 21.

90. Ibid, p 33.

GLOSSARY

• • •

ALCHEMY - Originally the art of making gold from base metals, but later a metaphor for of the transformation of unconscious material into higher consciousness.

ARCHETYPE - The primary behavioural and psychological characteristics specific to humanity and derived from universally recurrent themes, often carried by symbols and myth.

ASTROLOGY - The celestial art and science of determining the meaning of time.

CANON - An ancient esoteric law of measurement and proportion which regulated every aspect of human activity, including music, architecture, sculpture, astronomy and government.

CAPITAL - The cap of a column, often derived from vegetation forms such as the lotus or papyrus in Egypt and the acanthus in Greece and Rome.

CENTRE OF THE WORLD - In ancient cultures it was believed that the world had a centre, a navel, from which all measurements arose. These navels were often located in oracular centres and emanate from ancient Egypt.

CONSTELLATION - Series of stars identified by the ancients with animals, mythological beings and sacred objects. Twelve of the constellations along the ecliptic form the belt of the zodiac.

COSMIC EGG - An early image of the universe or the world as an egg enwrapped by a snake or serpent, symbolizing time.

COSMOLOGY - The central beliefs of a culture which often include science, astronomy, astrology and mythology.

CUBE - One of the Platonic Solids, symbolizing the physical world and earth.

ELEMENT - In ancient times the physical world was believed to be composed of the four elements of fire, earth, air and water.

EQUINOX - The two days each year when the sun crosses the equator and day is equal to night. The Spring Equinox is 0°Aries on about 21 March and the Autumn Equinox is 0°Libra on about 21 September.

GEMATRIA - The correlation of letters with numbers to obtain meaning, particularly in Greek and Hebrew languages. Each letter has a series of meanings and a number and words with the same sum have associated meanings.

GEODESY - A branch of mathematics which determines the exact positions of points and areas on the earth's surface and fluctuations of gravity and magnetism.

GEOMANCY - An art of divination using figures, lines or geographical features.

GEOMETRY - A branch of mathematics which deals with measurement, properties and relationships of points, lines, angles, surfaces and solids, but also an archetypal world of pure forms.

GNOMON - A rod or object used for measuring the position of the sun and hour of the day by its shadow.

GOLDEN MEAN or **GOLDEN SECTION** - The proportion phi (ϕ = 1:1.618) divides a line into two parts where the smaller is to the larger as the larger is to the whole. Phi describes the pattern of growth of spiral shells and certain flowers and other plants.

IDEAS - The transcendent forms or patterns of which existing things are imperfect representations.

LOGOS - The Word of God and the creative principle of the Universe.

LOTUS - A water plant which symbolizes the opening of the soul.

LUNAR MANSIONS - The Hindu astronomers/astrologers divided the zodiac belt into twenty-seven equal parts of $13\frac{1}{3}°$, which approximates the daily movement of the moon through the zodiac.

LUNAR MONTH - The time period from new moon to new moon, about 29.5 days.

MANDALA - A geometric projection (or psychocosmogram) of the world reduced to an essential pattern, used for contemplation or meditation, and a centring device for the psyche.

MATHEMATICS - The perfect and eternal principles of number and geometry which organize the physical universe.

MOUNTAIN - Symbolizes spiritual loftiness, generosity and the eternal nature of life. It is the place where heaven and earth meet, with its exterior the domain of the living and its interior the realm of the dead.

MYTH - A sacred and significant history which contains a moral truth and demonstrates images which describe the multi-faceted workings of the human spirit.

NUMBER - Transcendent and eternal mathematical ideas which form and regulate all natural processes.

ORIENTATION - The alignment of a megalith, monument or building in relation to the cardinal points, or the rising or setting of the sun, moon or stars.

PHI - The mathematical constant called the golden mean or golden section. (ϕ = 1:1.618)

PLATONIC SOLIDS - The five perfect regular shapes (cube, tetrahedron, octahedron, icosahedron and dodecahedron) which according to Plato correspond with the four elements and the universe.

PRECESSION OF THE EQUINOXES - Due to the wobbling of the earth's axis, its celestial equator moves in relation to the background stars, leading to an apparent movement backward through the signs of the zodiac at a rate of about one degree every 72 years.

PROPORTION - The relative dimensions of plane surfaces or interior spaces shown as a mathematical ratio. Therefore, the sides of a square are in the proportion of 1:1, of a cube 1:1:1, a double cube 1:1:2, and a triple square 1:3.

PYRAMID - A building form used originally in ancient Egypt which symbolizes the integration of the four elements or cardinal directions into a higher point of unity.

RELIGION - A linking back to the source of life and light.

SACRED - Contact with the absolute archetypal domain at the centre of reality, but outside of space and time.

SANCTUARY - Sacred place of psychic or spiritual safety, where religious observances are performed, and which reproduces the universe in its essence.

SIGN - A conventional image which possesses a definite meaning or significance.

SOLSTICE - The two days when day is longest and day is shortest during the year, at 0°Cancer (about 21 June) and at 0°Capricorn (about 21 December).

SPHERE - An image and symbol of the universe, heaven and the divine.

SPIRAL - An image of the creation and growth of the universe.

SPIRIT - The essence of light and life.

SQUARING THE CIRCLE - A geometric construction where a circle and a square with a common centre have the same circumference and periphery. The process symbolizes the integration of spiritual with earthly, or the creation of unity in the material world.

STUPA - A symbolic representation of the sacred mountain composed of shapes correlated with the four elements and the spirit.

SYMBOLISM - The art of thinking and creating in images which transcend the limitations of mind.

TEMPLE - An image of the celestial cosmos created on earth, a centre of the world, and an intersection between heaven and earth.

TREE OF LIFE - The pillar supporting heaven and the means by which the godhead descends to humanity and humanity ascends to the realm of the spirit.

VESICA PISCIS - A shape formed by two intersecting circles which symbolizes the female generative organ and also the place of integration of heaven and earth.

WHEEL - A symbol of the cycle of birth and death as the 'wheel of samsara', the cycle of the sun as a solar emblem, and the synthesis of cosmic forces and the passage of time.

WORLD AXIS (AXIS MUNDI) - The axis around which the earth rotates, but also a symbol of the intersection of heaven and earth, and the place where new souls enter the earth plane. Every temple or sacred city contains this meeting point between heaven, earth and hell.

WORLD TREE - A symbol of the life and structure of the cosmos, of the centre of the world, and the path through which the gods descend and mortals ascend to heaven.

ZODIAC - The ring of fixed constellations against which the sun, moon and planets move in the sky.

BIBLIOGRAPHY
• • •

(Dates in parenthesis are the original publication dates where of interest.)

ARDALAN, NADER AND LALEH BAKHTIAR, *The Sense of Unity: The Sufi Tradition in Persian Architecture*, University of Chicago, London, 1973.

ATKINSON, R. J. C., *Stonehenge and Avebury*, Dept.of Environment, London, 1976.

BLIGH BOND, FREDERICK, *Gematria*, RILKO/Thorsons, Wellingborough, 1977 (1917).

BRENNAN, MARTIN, *The Boyne Valley Vision*, Dolmen Press, Portlaoise, 1980. / *The Stars and The Stones: Ancient Art and Astronomy in Ireland*, Thames & Hudson, London, 1983.

BURCKHARDT, TITUS, *Sacred Art in East and West*, Perennial, London, 1967.

BURL, AUBREY, *Prehistoric Avebury*, Yale University, New Haven, 1979.

CAMPBELL, JOSEPH AND ROBERTS, RICHARD, *Tarot Revelations*, Vernal Equinox Press, San Anselmo, 1982.

CHARPENTIER, LOUIS, *The Mysteries of Chartres Cathedral*, RILKO, London, 1972.

CHU, W. K., AND SHERRILL, W. A. *The Astrology of I Ching*, Routledge & Kegan Paul, London, 1976.

CIRCLOT, J E, *A Dictionary of Symbols*, Routledge, London, 1988.

COLEGRAVE, SUKIE, *The Spirit of the Valley: Androgyny and Chinese Thought*, Virago, London, 1979.

COWEN, PAINTON, *Rose Windows*, Thames & Hudson, London, 1979.

CRITCHLOW, KEITH, *Time Stands Still*, Gordon Frazer, London, 1979./ 'Chartres Maze', *Architectural Association Quarterly*, vol. 5, no. 2. / with Jane Carroll and Vaughan Lee, Llewylyn, *Chartres: A Model of the Universe?*, RILKO, Cambridge, 1975.

CROWLEY, ALEISTER, *The Kabbalah of Aleister Crowley*, Samuel Weiser, New York, 1973 (1909).

DAVIDSON, D., AND ALDERSMITH, H., *The Great Pyramid: Its Divine Message*, Williams and Norgate, London, 1925.

DAWKINS, PETER, *Arcadia: The Ancient Egyptian Mysteries*, Francis Bacon Research Trust, Stratford-on-Avon, 1988.

EDGAR, MORTON, *The Great Pyramid: Its Time Features*, Bone & Hulley, Glasgow, 1924.

EITEL, REV. E. J., *Feng Shui: Natural Science in China*, Cokaygne, Cambridge, 1973 (1873).

FLUDD, ROBERT, trans. Patricia Tahil, *The Origin and Structure of the Cosmos*, Magnum Opus, Edinburgh, 1982.

GETTINGS, FRED, *The Secret Zodiac: The Hidden Art in Medieval Astrology*, Routledge & Kegan Paul, London, 1983.

HADINGHAM, EVAN, *Early Man and the Cosmos*, William Heinemann, London, 1983.

HALL, MANLY P., *The Secret Teachings of All Ages*, Philosophical Research Society, Los Angeles, 1968 (1928).

HAND, ROBERT, 'Astrology as a Revolutionary Science', in *The Future of Astrology*, Unwin Hyman, London, 1987.

HAWKINS, GERALD S. and WHITE, JOHN B., *Stonehenge Decoded*, Doubleday, New York, 1965.

HEGGIE, DOUGLAS C., *Megalithic Science*, Thames & Hudson, London, 1981.

HUNTLEY, H. E., *The Divine Proportion*, Dover, New York, 1970.

JUNG, EMMA, and VON FRANZ, M.-L., *The Grail Legend*, G. P. Putnam, New York, 1970.

JUNG, CARL. G., ed., with VON FRANZ, M.-L., JOSEPH HENDERSON, JOLANDE JACOBI, ANIELA JAFF, *Man and His Symbols*, Anchor Books, New York, 1964. / *Word and Image*, edited by Aniela Jaffe, Princeton University Press, Princeton, 1979.

KASAS, SAVAS, *Important Medical Centres in Antiquity: Epidaurus and Corinth*, Editions Kasas, Athens, 1979.

KIDSON, PETER, *Romansk- og Gotisk Kunst*, Lademann, Copenhagen, 1970.

KRUPP, DR. E. C., *Echoes of Ancient Skies: The Astronomy of Lost Civilizations*, Harper & Row, New York, 1983.

LAWLOR, ROBERT, *Sacred Geometry*, Thames & Hudson, London, 1982.

LETHABY, WILLIAM, *Architecture, Mysticism and Myth*, Architectural Press, London, 1974 (1891).

LIP, EVELYN, *Feng Shui for Business*, Times Books International, Singapore, 1976.

LOVE, JEFF, *The Quantum Gods*, Compton Russell Element, Tisbury, 1976.

MACGREGOR MATHERS, S. L., *The Kabbalah Unveiled*, Routledge & Kegan Paul, London, 1970 (1926).

MANN, A. T., *Life*Time Astrology*, Element, Shaftesbury, 1991 (1984). / *Millennium Prophecies*, Element, Shaftesbury, 1992. / *The Divine Plot: Astrology and Reincarnation*, Element, Shaftesbury, 1991 (1986). / Editor, *The Future of Astrology*, Unwin Hyman, London, 1987. / *The Mandala Astrological Tarot*, Macmillan, London, 1987. / *The Round Art: The Astrology of Time and Space*, Dragon's World, London, 1977. / *Twelve Mandalas*, Dragons World, 1976.

MARC, OLIVIER, *Psychology of the House*, Thames & Hudson, London, 1977.

MICHELL, JOHN, *Ancient Metrology*, Pentacle, London, 1981. / *The City of Revelation*, Garnstone, London, 1972. / *The View Over Atlantis*, Garnstone, London, 1969.

MYER, ISAAC, Qabbalah: *The Philosophical Writings of Avicebron*, Stuart & Watkins, London, 1970 (1888).

NASR, SEYYED HUSSEIN, *Islamic Science*, World of Islam Festival, London, 1976.

NEWHAM, C. A., *The Astronomical Significance of Stonehenge*, John Blackburn, Leeds, 1972.

NITSCHKE, GÜNTER, *The Architecture of the Japanese Garden*, Benedikt Taschen, Köln, 1991.

NUTTGENS, PATRICK, *The Story of Architecture*, Phaidon, Oxford, 1983.

O'KELLY, CLAIRE, *Illustrated Guide to Newgrange and other Boyne Monuments*, O'Kelly, Cork, 1978.

PEARSON, DAVID, *The Natural House Book*, Conran Octopus, London,

PENNICK, NIGEL, *The Ancient Science of Geomancy*, Thames & Hudson, London, 1979.

PFEIFFER, BRUCE BROOKS, *Frank Lloyd Wright*, Benedikt Taschen, Köln, 1991.

RHIE, MARYLIN AND THURMAN, ROBERT, *Wisdom and Compassion: The Sacred Art of Tibet*, Royal Academy of Arts, London, 1992.

ROSSBACH, SARAH, *Feng Shui*, Rider, London, 1984.

SANTILLANA, GIORGIO and VON DECHEND, HERTHA, *Hamlet's Mill*, Godine, Boston, 1977.

SAUNDERS, MICHAEL, 'Stonehenge Planetarium,' RILKO Newsletter, No. 21, Winter 1982, and Downs Books, Caterham, 1979.

SCHWALLER DE LUBICZ, ISHA, *The Opening of the Way*, trans. Rupert Gleadow, Inner Traditions, New York, 1981.

SCHWALLER DE LUBICZ, R. A., *Sacred Science*, trans. A. & G. VandenBroeck, Inner Traditions International, New York, 1982 (1961)./ *Symbol and Symbolic*, trans. Deborah & Robert Lawlor, Autumn Press, Brookline, 1979 (1949)./ *The Temple in Man: The Secrets of Ancient Egypt*, trans. Deborah & Robert Lawlor, Autumn Press, Brookline, 1977 (1949).

SKINNER, STEPHEN, *The Living Earth Manual of Feng-Shui*, Routledge & Kegan Paul, London, 1982.

SMYTH, PIAZZI, *Our Inheritance in the Great Pyramid*, Isbister, London, 1880.

SPENGLER, OSWALD, *The Decline of the West*, George Allen & Unwin, 1971 (1926 and 1928).

STIRLING, WILLIAM, *The Canon, An Exposition of the Pagan Myth Perpetuated in the Cabala as a Rule of All the Arts*, RILKO/Thorsons, Wellingborough, 1981 (1897).

SWAN, JAMES A., *Sacred Places*, Bear & Co, Santa Fe, 1990.

TEMPLE, ROBERT K. G., *The Sirius Mystery*, Sidgwick & Jackson, London, 1976.

THOMPSON, ANGEL, *Feng Shui*, (unpublished mss.), Los Angeles, 1992.

TOMPKINS, PETER, *Mysteries of the Mexican Pyramids*, Thames & Hudson, London, 1976. / *Secrets of the Great Pyramid*, Harper & Row, New York, 1971.

TUCCI, GIUSEPPE, *The Theory and Practice of the Mandala*, Rider, London, 1971.

UNDERWOOD, GUY, *The Pattern of the Past*, Abacus, London, 1973.

VANDENBROECK, ANDRÉ, *Al-Kemi: A Memoir of R. A. Schwaller de Lubicz*, Lindisfarne, Hudson, 1987.

VON FRANZ, MARIE-LOUISE, *Number and Time*, Rider, London, 1974.

WATKINS, ALFRED, *The Old Straight Track*, Abacus, London, 1975 (1925).

WEAVER, HERBERT, *Divining the Primary Sense: Unfamiliar Radiation in Nature, Art and Science*, Routledge & Kegan Paul, London, 1978.

WEST, JOHN ANTHONY, *Serpent in the Sky*, Harper & Row, New York, 1979./ *The Traveler's Key to Ancient Egypt*, Alfred A. Knopf, New York, 1985.

WESTLAKE, DR. AUBREY T., *The Pattern of Health*, Shambhala, Boulder, 1973.

WILHELM, RICHARD, (trans.), *The I Ching, or Book of Changes*, Bollingen, Princeton, 1971 (1950)./ *The Secret of the Golden Flower*, Routledge & Kegan Paul, London, 1969 (1931).

YATES, FRANCES, *The Art of Memory*, Peregrine, London, 1966. *Giordano Bruno and the Hermetic Tradition*, Routledge & Kegan Paul, London, 1971. / *The Rosicrucian Enlightenment*, Paladin, London, 1975. / *The Theatre of the World*, Routledge & Kegan Paul, London, 1969.

ZIMMER, ERICH, *Rudolf Steiner Als Architekt Von Wohn- und Zweckbauten*, Verlag Freies Geistesleben, Basel, 1985.

ZIMMER, HEINRICH, *Myths and Symbols in Indian Art and Civilization*, ed. JOSEPH CAMPBELL, Bollingen Series VI, Pantheon, Washington, 1946.